Meeting the Challenges of
Being a Single Mom

GOING
IT
ALONE

Michele Howe

HENDRICKSON
PUBLISHERS

GOING
IT
ALONE

Going It Alone
© 1999 by Michele Howe

Published by Hendrickson Publishers
140 Summit Street
Peabody, MA 01960

ISBN: 1-56563-452-7

First printing: September 1999

Cover design by Veldheer Creative Services, Byron Center, Mich.
Interior design and typesetting by Pilcrow Book Services, Kirkland, Wash.
Edited by Judy Bodmer and Heather Stroobosscher

Dedication

To my friends Sarah and Mary
who faced an uncertain future
with courage and integrity.

Every woman should be as blessed
as I am to have friends like you.

⌒⌒ Table of Contents

Acknowledgements

While writing this book, I came to appreciate just how difficult an editor's job can be. Dan Penwell, Hendrickson's trade product manager, recognized a felt need and matched it with a plan to meet this need. He envisioned how he could translate my thoughts and feelings into words that would help, encourage, and give hope to my readers. He worked with me until both he and I had the same vision for this book. Dan is not only astute in his observations and suggestions, but also balances his criticisms with consistent and ongoing encouragement. He challenges those who work with him to achieve excellence. Because he expects good things, he's likely to get excellence.

This book was a labor of love for my friends who are single moms. I am thankful that Dan gave me the opportunity to work with him on this project. His direction was essential; his affirmation, bountiful; and I am indebted to Dan for the lessons I've learned. I'm also grateful to Scott Pinzon, Judy Bodmer, and Heather Stroobosscher, who worked with me in the editing and rewriting and rewriting and rewriting. Scott promised me, "You learn a lot on every writing project—we all do." He was right! To all four of my editors, thank you for showing patience, tact, and countless kindnesses to this novice book writer.

✍ Introduction

Some years ago, a close friend called to ask me if I thought her marriage was in trouble. Within a few months, my friend wasn't wondering any longer. She knew. About that same time, another close friend called with the news of her own impending divorce. Both of these women found themselves facing life and parenting on their own.

At the time, their pain of abandonment felt like death to all who loved them. This heavy chain of unresolved emotions, of dreams and broken promises, left my friends and their children in agonizing pain. Together we wept. One day led to another, weeks turned to months, and months to years. Eventually, healing found root in their hearts and lives. But time alone did not soften the blows. Jesus Christ and his redemptive power at work in my friends' lives did. In ways I can only describe as miraculous, God brought completeness and genuine healing to these moms and their children.

Today, my friends and their children are thriving, not circumstantially, but providentially. Each day continues to bring new trials and struggles as they labor to make their houses into homes where God is Lord. The fruit of their labor has already multiplied in the hearts of their children and those whom they influence.

Single mom, this book was written in celebration of you. My prayer is that this text, born of the pain carried by other single moms, will bring help and healing along the way.

O LORD my God, I called to you for help and you healed me. . . . You turned my wailing into dancing; you removed my sackcloth and clothed me with joy, that my heart may sing to you and not be silent. O LORD my God, I will give you thanks forever (Ps. 30:2, 11–12).

1

Tough Times:

When Kids Face Their Pain

*L*isa's life was turned inside out when she was awarded full custody of her daughter Katie. If it wasn't a physical need she was tending, it was an emotional one. Lisa's energy was devoted to seeing that food was on the table and that Katie had enough clean clothes for the next day. Any plans Lisa had for helping her daughter cope with her dad's absence were soon forgotten in the day-to-day activities of life.

Every morning at 4:30 the alarm clock rings insistently. As Lisa reaches over to turn it off, she's reminded of how she used to reach across her sleeping husband, Craig, to get another five minutes of rest. She also remembers how nice it was to snuggle in Craig's arms before arising. Now, instead of relishing an extra few minutes to sleep, Lisa senses another sort of alarm going off inside her head. She feels afraid.

Lisa is afraid of a future without any loving support from her ex-spouse. She is afraid of learning to make all the decisions on her own. In short, Lisa is afraid of living. So, for the next five minutes, she pulls the covers up to her chin and weeps.

Reluctantly, Lisa dries her tears and wills herself out of bed and into the shower. Her job at a local bakery forces her to overcome her natural tendency to stay up late and sleep in the next morning. For the last four months, Lisa has tried to get in bed right after Katie does at 9:30 P.M. But it doesn't matter because she doesn't sleep. Her grief and sadness exhaust her during the day and haunt her at night.

As Lisa wearily readies herself for work, she sets out Katie's lunch near her schoolbooks. She peeks in at Katie one last time and mentally checks off her list—alarm is set for 6:00 A.M., clothes are out, home-work's by the door, lunch is packed. Okay, Lisa reassures herself, Katie's only home alone for one hour in the morning. She will call her at 6:30 to make sure she's up. She frets about forgetting because she sometimes gets busy rolling out bread dough and icing cakes. Lisa locks the door and checks it twice. She reminds herself to talk to Katie again tonight about her dad's visit on Sunday. She's been so withdrawn again these past few days. Thus, Lisa starts another day.

As Lisa discovered, single parenting is all about facing past hurts, dealing with present fears, and building a future full of promise while simultaneously coping with life's everyday pressures. For Lisa and her daughter, the ebb and flow of life changed drastically with Lisa's divorce.

Before her divorce, Lisa was a stay-at-home wife and mother. She ordered her days by making to-do lists and working through each item. By the time Katie arrived home from school, they had two hours for girl talk, craft projects, and relaxed dinner preparation prior to Craig's coming home from work at the office.

But following the divorce, Lisa found herself still working to accomplish the tasks on her list (when she had the time to write one) when she arrived home from the bakery. She had to juggle errands with dinner, housework, homework, and bedtime. It's no wonder that Katie sometimes got irritated with her mom's lack of willingness to simply sit down and chat about the day's events. But Lisa's work schedule didn't seem to quit. One day filled with demanding responsibilities ushered in the next.

Both Katie and Lisa felt cheated. They wanted their life back the way it was before Craig left and they knew it wasn't going to happen. So Lisa worked herself to a frazzle trying to hold hearth and home together. She worked at the bakery, worked at home, and worked to forget all the pain the man she once loved has caused her and her daughter. Katie, on the other hand, was simply consumed with grief. She couldn't shake the overwhelming sadness she felt when she looked at the table set for two instead of three and realized for the umpteenth time that her dad wasn't going to walk in the door for dinner.

On better days, Lisa and Katie were able to share a tenuous laugh together over dinner. But most of the time, they hurt so much that smiling wasn't an option. Consumed by grief, both mother and daughter considered it an accomplishment to endure another day.

Parents like Lisa must be available to help their children work through their grief so they can all move toward true acceptance of their new family unit. Children like Katie eventually have to accept that their life as they once knew it is forever gone. As both the parent and child accept their losses and stop trying to fight against the changes, inner healing can slowly take place.

Once Lisa and Katie gradually felt their way through their anger and sadness, they were more able to accept their situation. In practical terms, Lisa eventually learned to make time to repeatedly listen to her daughter's thoughts and views and empathize with her in meaningful ways. As Lisa learned, moving ahead in an effort to build a strong, single parent family unit became easier after old hurts had been properly addressed. Lisa and Katie spent many nights rehashing the divorce and all the problems that had led up to it. Lisa considers it a blessing that she and her daughter were able to face their pain together and subsequently start their healing as a team.

As Lisa and Katie realized, once a family has embarked on this great adventure of single parent family living, putting into practice new coping strategies made a significant difference in their ability to face their days with courage.

Perhaps you experienced challenges similar to those Lisa faced. Maybe you've been forced to return to work, adjust your schedule, change your priorities, and set different standards. While every divorce scenario is made up of unique components, lifestyle changes are inevitable. It's up to you to make deliberate plans to build a new life for your family. The following list of suggestions includes ideas for helping children cope with grief which have already been tried by other single moms. Be encouraged; with God's help, hope and healing are not only possible but promised.

Ways to Help Your Child Grieve

• **Grieve in order to heal.** The grieving process is characterized by denial, anger, bargaining (what ifs), sadness and depression, resolution, and then forgiveness. Unfortunately, children do not have the skills to articulate these emotions in the precise manner grownups utilize. So help your children identify their feelings as normal and be ready to share your heart with them. Let them know they are accepted even though their emotions may be volatile at times. Above all, give your children time to grieve the loss they feel so keenly. Don't rush or prod them in an attempt to "get this over with" so you can get on with your lives. Both adults and children must spend adequate time working through this step-by-step grieving process. Grieving is not wasted time, it's growing time.

Rebekah did this by instituting a "crying time." Every Friday before dinner, she and her kids gathered in the living room and talked about how each one was doing. They each vented frustrations and even cried on occasion. Then they dried their eyes, hugged one another, and went in to dinner. This short time of weekly assessment offered emotional release. Over a period of months, the crying time transformed itself into a weekly family meeting time when accomplishments and celebrations were shared.

• **Develop new traditions as a family.** Discuss new creative activities you and your children would like to incorporate during upcoming celebrations, such as birthdays, holidays, and vacations. Think of some things you always wanted to try but haven't gotten around to doing. Go caroling and hand out cookies at Christmas, join a summer bowling league, or try making a birthday piñata. Don't wait for a special event to try something different. How about designating every Thursday evening as family fun night? Order a pizza. Get out the board games. Watch a video and relax.

After Crissy and her husband divorced, her kids no longer had anyone to roller-skate with through the neighborhood. At a used sporting goods store, Crissy bought Rollerblades and pads for her knees, elbows, and wrists. Within a week, she was able to keep up with her ten- and eleven-year-old daughters on their in-line skates. Crissy's daughters were thrilled to have Mom along for the fun.

• **Make use of available resources.** Take a trip to your local Christian book store. Ask your church librarian or pastor for reference books dealing with single parenting issues. Look for materials to read with your children. Then discuss questions and answers together. Share the experience of seeing each situation through the positive viewpoint found in God's Word. Study various issues of particular interest to your children. Topics may include: loneliness, hopelessness, anger, grief, sexuality, finances, and goal-setting.

Tracy passed the word around at her local church that she wanted any resource books appropriate for her and the kids to read together. Another single mom heard of Tracy's need and gathered helpful books, videos, and tapes she had used several years earlier. Before long, Tracy's confidence as a single mom blossomed as she learned to address her children's issues of concern with knowledge and understanding.

• **Use the written word to work through feelings.** Purchase diaries, one for you and one for each child. Set aside time once a week to write down feelings, thoughts, and ideas. Take thirty minutes to journal and reminisce over the past week. Mentally review the different events and how you and your children responded to them. Communicate to your children that journaling is a way of getting out thoughts they might not have taken time to really think through. After you've finished, put the books away, bring out the hot cocoa and don't be surprised if your child opens the lines of communication with one or two questions or thoughts.

Lonnie bribed her two sons into journaling on a weekly basis. She offered them dinner at McDonald's or Burger King for every half hour they spent writing in their journals. Lonnie's boys have filled three journals in two years and the cashier at the local McDonald's has gotten to know Lonnie's family by name.

• **Use your memory to build a hopeful future.** Buy a scrapbook, get out the Bible, and select a "life verse" for your family. Choose a verse which will fortify your family during troubled times and bring joy during blessed events. Write this verse in the front cover of the scrapbook. Sally and her children selected a life verse from the book of Isaiah. They decorated their scrapbook with photos of each of them participating in their favorite activities. Each time one of them reached a new goal, won an award, or enjoyed a family fun event, they made a note of the date and the event. Then they inserted photos, ticket stubs, awards, and anything else that helped them recall what a great experience they'd had.

Write down funny sayings or make mention of God's provision under each item to help recall any fuzzy memories. As you work on this project, opportunities to reminisce will naturally unfold hidden tears and laughter. The scrapbook itself will remain a tangible reminder of a past filled with good times too. It also gives the child a visible foundation on which to build a happier future.

- **Reach out to others in need.** In your family's pain, extend yourself to others who are hurting or needy. Befriend the lonely and set an example of giving for your children to pattern themselves after.

On their way to church, Margaret would sometimes see an elderly man slowly walking the half mile from his bus stop to their church building. One Sunday, she stopped to offer him a ride to the church and then invited him to their apartment for lunch. Over time, Margaret's kids found they had a new "adopted" grandfather to love and fuss over. Reaching out need not be extravagant or costly. It only demands small bits of time given in loving service.

- **Use hands-on activities to encourage inner healing.** Consider the benefit of a pet or a new hobby. Time spent loving an animal or developing a personal skill takes energy and concentration. Your children need to focus on areas outside the family and the current transitional pain it brings. Give your children the help they need to experience satisfaction in a job well done. Assist them in finding their niches, whether it be learning to care for an animal or developing the newest Rollerblade moves.

Teri's idea of a pet wasn't a four-foot-long iguana. But her son Todd had done his research as she requested. So, Teri's home now includes herself, her son Todd, and their iguana, Menace.

- **Be open to the helpful input of others.** Laurie's nearest relations lived over a thousand miles away. Her friends were as busy as she was. At the suggestion of her Sunday school teacher, Laurie made an appointment with one of the pastors of her local church for help in handling a problem with her seventeen-year-old daughter, Kelly. Laurie's pastor spent time alone with Laurie one week, brought Kelly in by herself the next week, then finally counseled them together. During those sessions, Laurie and Kelly learned to respect their differences without allowing them to deteriorate into fighting matches. Both mother and daughter learned how to accept each other.

If your children have needs you cannot meet it does not signal defeat or weakness. Rather, seeking support from those who hold a significant place in your children's lives reveals a humble heart and the godly perseverance so necessary in developing a mature family life.

Written Resources to Strengthen Your Family

- *Love Is a Choice*
  Drs. Hemfelt, Minirth, Meier. Nelson.

- *Shepherding a Child's Heart*
  Tedd Tripp. Shepherd Press.

- *Hide and Seek*
  Dr. James Dobson. Fleming H. Revell.

- *Raising Positive Kids in a Negative World*
  Zig Ziglar. Oliver-Nelson.

- *Kids Who Carry Our Pain*
  Dr. R. Hemfelt and Dr. P. Warren. Nelson.

- *Nobody Likes Me: Helping Your Child Make Friends*
  Elaine McEwan. Harold Shaw.

2

Overcoming Jealousy:

Helping Kids from

Single Parent Homes Cope

*T*welve-year-old Jillian slammed down the phone. She couldn't believe her friends were actually going to attend the turn-about dance at school. Jillian wanted to scream. All of their dads would be happy to take them. Not her dad, though. He'd make some excuse like he always did. Jillian held back her tears as she doodled on the phone pad. As her mom, Cheryl, walked into the room, Jillian continued to mumble about her dad's unreliability. The more Jill mumbled, the more angry she felt.

"Jillian, what did you just say?" her mother asked in disbelief.

"I said, I hate him and I wish he was dead!" Jillian sobbed as the tears flowed down her cheeks.

"You can't mean that, Honey. He's still your dad."

"Well, if he's still my dad, why isn't he here like my friends' fathers?" Jillian shouted.

"Sit down, Jill, we need to talk this out."

"Why? Talking didn't stop you and Daddy from getting a divorce!"

"Please, tell me why you're so upset."

"Everyone I know is going to the turn-about dance at school," Jillian said. "Everyone except me."

"Jill, why don't you ask your dad to take you? If he isn't on the road, I'm sure he'd love to go with you."

"Right, Mom. Just like he wanted to go camping with us last summer."

"Honey, your dad and I were already separated by the time our summer camping trip rolled around. The problem was between your dad and me, not you. Your dad was willing to take you alone. Don't you remember?" Cheryl asked.

"I guess, but I didn't want to go with him after he left!" Jill cried.

"Come over here, Jill." Cheryl pulled her daughter into her arms.

Cheryl finds herself constantly uttering words of praise about her ex-husband Mark. Though the sentiments stick in her throat, she knows her daughter Jillian needs to hear some positive words about her dad. "I never thought I'd be the one singing Mark's praises to another living soul," Cheryl says. Surprised by her daughter's anger and aggressive attitudes, Cheryl feels shell-shocked. Not only is Cheryl trying to recover and regroup from her nine-month-old divorce, she also feels the burden of her daughter's downhill emotional state weighing heavily on her. "It's up to me," she says, "to get Jill through this fiasco. But, the truth is, I feel as bad as she does. I'm angry too. I'm sometimes jealous of friends who are still married." Tormented by her own feelings, Cheryl wonders if somehow her own anger has transferred to her daughter.

Cheryl has a right to worry. Jillian's inner frustration is continually fueled by circumstances beyond her control. It seems like the most insignificant events become tragic reminders of how she and her mom are now alone. Jillian frequently gets that queasy sick feeling in the pit of her stomach whenever she hears her friends talk about their dads. It's especially painful when her friends go on vacation or out to dinner as a family. Jill also recalls times when having Dad around made their life a lot less complicated. Several weeks ago, the car broke down while Cheryl was driving her to the season's final soccer game. Cheryl and Jillian ended up having to wait two hours for the tow truck to come and haul the car to the repair shop. "It's bad enough to miss out on the fun stuff with Dad," Jillian complained, "but now his being gone made me miss my last school soccer game, too. Since Mom and Dad got divorced, Dad's not here to take care of the car or fix things when they break."

For Jillian, every area of her life has been touched by her dad's absence. Friends, family, school, hobbies—no area remains unscathed by her parents' divorce. As an only child, Jillian was used to getting what she wanted. She wasn't necessarily spoiled; she was, however, doted upon by both Mom and Dad. But since her dad's been gone, Jillian's now more accustomed to the word no. If a constraint isn't monetary, it's time-related. Jillian doesn't understand that Cheryl is doing her level best to maintain life as they once knew it.

Jillian's friends are another sore point with her. Even if her friends could understand what she's going through, they don't articulate their feelings in a way that suits Jill. She feels sorry for herself and she's not about to let go of her anger. In Jill's subconscious, her negative emotions are her final walls of protection against further pain and disappointment.

Last weekend, Jillian's best friend, Angie, invited her to a big sleep-over. Jill was delighted. She wanted to have some fun with her friends and forget about Dad and Mom's divorce for awhile. The evening started out like an answer to prayer. Good food, great CDs, juicy secrets, and giggles over the new guy at school. Jillian was having a terrific time until the subject of the Father/Daughter Turn-About Dance came up. When her friends asked Jill if she was going to invite her dad, Jillian's face got beet red as she angrily responded, "No! And don't bring it up again." Stunned by her reaction, Jillian's friends tip-toed around her for the rest of the evening. Gone were the silly jokes and the knowing looks shared among intimate friends. Gone was the fun Jillian had so desired. Worst of all, Jill knew it was her fault.

The next morning, Jillian came home two hours earlier than expected. It didn't take a genius to figure out that something was wrong. Cheryl spent the rest of the morning trying to get Jillian to open up. After Cheryl's third cup of coffee, and Jillian's half dozen or so Oreo cookies, the tears finally came. Holding her daughter tightly, Cheryl reassured Jillian that they'd both be okay. "But you don't know how mad I get," Jillian sobbed, "I'm mad at everybody, not just Daddy."

"I know exactly how you feel, Jill," Cheryl said. "But sometimes just admitting we have a problem is how we start learning to overcome it."

Cheryl and Jillian had hit their crisis point. Once they did, they summoned the strength and determination to forge ahead. Both mother and daughter had expected to be a lot more stable this many months after the divorce. But in the beginning, Cheryl hadn't realized how deeply hurt her daughter was. It took Jillian's angry outbursts to jar Cheryl from her own emotional state of limbo and into action.

When parents divorce, the adults aren't the only ones who are angry. In fact, if you look around at families in crisis, it's obvious that the kids suffer as much if not more than their parents. This pain continues to manifest itself in many ways. Some ways are subtle and easily overlooked. Others are not so subtle and in Jillian's case, definitely not silent.

Cheryl remembers the hour Mark exited the home and a void entered. Neither Cheryl nor Jillian were able to escape the feeling that someone was missing. Jillian was keenly aware of this loss every time she visited a friend's home whose parents were still married. Or when her schoolmates talked about the school turn-about dance they were anticipating. At every turn, Jillian had to face and accept her family's new status: that of a fatherless, single parent home.

It's no wonder that many young people from single parent homes become depressed and often envious of their friends who enjoy the security of living with two parents in love and committed to each other.

If you are newly divorced, a divorce veteran, or about to join the single parenting ranks, your children will face similar circumstances. Despite the overwhelming pain experienced by families going through divorce, there are practical steps you can take to help you and your family make the adjustment healthier and less traumatic. As you and your children feel your way through the volatile and emotional abandonment issues brought on by divorce, the following suggestions may help soften this time of transition. You'll find the path to healthy adjustment far less injurious than hanging onto any residual anger and jealousy.

Steps Toward Adjusting to Divorce

• **Discard the "perfect family" myth**. Tread lightly yet with conviction as you explain to your children that even families with two parents have problems. You might cite incidents of overwork, illness, lack of money, sexual abuse, physical violence, infidelity, drug and alcohol abuse, or emotional illnesses as examples of problems common to two-parent families. Encourage your children to be thankful they haven't experienced such horrors. Or if they have, help them to be grateful they are removed from those situations now.

Bari's four boys were always complaining about their lack of money. Bari decided to take her sons to see those who were in real monetary difficulties. She signed the five of them up to serve food at their church's soup kitchen. After several hours of serving food and cleaning up for the homeless men and women of their city, Bari's sons weren't so quick to gripe the next time Bari had to say no to a new purchase.

• **Instill the principle of God as the father to the fatherless.** Sonya's kids weren't going to have much of a Christmas this year. Instead of feeling sorry for herself, Sonya brought her kids into the kitchen where they prayed for God to meet their needs. With a lighter heart, Sonya went to bed. The following morning, she went out to her car and found two bags of groceries, two bags of good used clothing, and a generous gift certificate to a local store.

"A father to the fatherless . . . is God in his holy dwelling" (Ps. 68:5). God has promised to step in and provide for the widows and orphans in a special way. His Word says he will provide for all the needs of a child of divorce. Ask your child to commit this verse to memory with you.

• **Relate that all people have "empty heart places" that cause pain.** Divorce is not the only change which brings loss. Death separates loved ones. Job relocation tears families and friends apart. Even growing and changing as an individual can bring loss of relationship. Explain that every person must accept their losses as part of life. Emphasize to your children that they are not alone in their feelings of sadness or emptiness.

Calling her kids together, Denise explained her decision to contact a nearby children's home. Now each week, Denise and her family bring a six-year-old orphaned boy home for the afternoon. She loves watching her kids loving little Eric—playing with him, giving him snacks, and just loving him. Her kids quickly recognized how much they still had and what they had to offer others.

• **Share biblically the results of being jealous of friends who have two parents.** Gently remind your children that while feeling jealous is understandable, you still expect them to work through their negative feelings. Explain that the Bible tells us nothing good comes from nursing jealous and bitter emotions. It can tear apart the friendships and relationships we treasure the most.

• **Encourage married couples and friends of the opposite sex to visit.** Once a month, Nora invites a family from church over for dinner. Her boys look forward to the rough-housing that the husbands offer and Nora simply delights in providing her family and friends with a good meal and friendly conversation.

Let your married friends become involved in your children's lives so they can see other healthy families interact. Your children will find comfort regarding their own faults and imperfections as they observe others living honestly, making mistakes, and subsequently forgiving each other. Perhaps most importantly, your children will witness other adults hanging in there even through the tough times.

• **Make the most of the time available with the noncustodial parent.** Help your children to have healthy, realistic attitudes toward the absent parent. Comments like, "Your dad still loves you. He just has some problems he needs to work out," will impart the freedom for your children to love their father. You want to free your children from any guilt they may experience because of torn allegiance between you and your ex-spouse.

Angela followed this advice and now sets aside two afternoons a week to shop and run errands. Her ex-husband, Mike, drives right over from his job on those afternoons to spend time with the children. Angela feels better knowing her kids are in a safe environment and she is able to get her errands done as well. The children benefit by having interaction with both parents throughout the week.

• **Use feelings of anger, jealousy, and bitterness as a springboard to help others.** After some of your children's pain has dissipated, challenge them to view their friends, family, and neighbors from a new and loving perspective. Help them to probe their feelings and recall how vulnerable they feel at times. Then help them to look for opportunities to show love to others when they sense others are struggling.

When the kids arrive home from school, Joann is ready with a snack for them. While they munch, she listens. Joann knows more about her children's classmates than the teacher probably does. As her kids fill her in on what's happening in the fourth and fifth grade classes, she makes mental notes. Then, after their snack, both Joann and her kids pray for those children whose needs were discussed.

3
Fortified Family:
Developing Healthy Interdependence

Simultaneously, four alarm clocks went off in the Grant household. In thirteen-year-old Corey's room, the music from a clock radio played softly. A television's early morning news program was heard from eleven-year-old Ian's room. And in nine-year-old Jeremy's room, the shrill dinging of an old fashioned bell clock shook the walls. In Kim's room, her grandmother's antique cuckoo clock majestically opened its door and a minuscule bird sang its chirping song a single time and then silently retreated back inside its domain.

Kim groaned. How she longed to sleep in on this spring morning. But in a last-ditch attempt to get caught up around the house, she'd laid down the law to her three kids the night before. "Everybody set your alarms for 7:30 A.M.," she'd told them at last night's dinner table. "We're getting up early and we're going to work until everything's done. We *will* work all day if we have to so that this house is in shape before your grandparents come next weekend."

As Kim's three boys looked around the house, they winced. Mom meant business this time and it scared them. They shuddered as they allowed their eyes to take in the overgrown weeds and grass, the windows covered with fingerprints and smudges, the cobwebs and dust bunnies taking over their home. Their minds wandered for just a few moments before Mom's voice beckoned them back to reality. "All right, Corey, since you're the oldest, you'll do the yard work. I want the dead branches heaped on the burn pile. I want the flower beds weeded. Make sure you don't leave clumps of dead weeds and dirt lying on the ground either. Take them back to the compost pile next to my garden. Then you'll need to cut the grass.

"Ian, I want you to sort all the clothes, according to light and dark colors, remember? You'll be in charge of washing clothes and drying them. Be sure you spray spot remover on any stains before you toss the clothes into the machine. Just put the folded clothes on everyone's beds. Oh, while the clothes are washing, scrub out the refrigerator and use hot, soapy water to clean those sticky grates. Got it?

"Jeremy, you'll be working along side me tomorrow. We'll tackle the sweeping, dusting, and bathrooms first. Then after lunch, we'll take down the curtains and clean the windows and sills," Kim had explained. "Well, guys, I think that about covers it. Go on outside before it gets dark. You may even have enough time to play ball before the mosquitoes get too thick."

Kicking at the stones beneath their feet, all three boys looked the picture of perfect misery. "Play ball? Who wants to play ball after hearing that?" Corey said.

"It isn't fair. Why should we have to work on Saturday? It's our only day off from school," Ian complained.

Jeremy walked behind his two older brothers kicking at stones, too. Jeremy's despair was not, however, about all the forthcoming work. He was wondering where his dad was right then and why he didn't come home. If his dad loved them like he said he did, why didn't he come home to stay?

Inside the kitchen, Kim placed the last dirty dish inside the dishwasher. As she poured the detergent into the dispenser, she sighed. It was going to be a long weekend. What was she thinking? There had to be some way to keep up with all this work. But how? She was barely able to keep pace with the boys' schedules during the week. Between working and running them to their games, she just didn't have much time left, let alone the energy to accomplish it all. She felt guilty even asking the boys to help. It wasn't their fault she and Jerry had divorced.

As Kim plopped down on the couch and watched for her sons to come home from the ball field, she realized she needed a plan. That was it! The Grant family needed a game plan. Her boys were certainly up to their ears in sports. So, she'd appeal to their sense of team spirit. The more she thought about it, the more it looked like it would work. She'd build one mighty invincible team out of the four Grants.

Kim developed a workable, organized plan for maintaining the household. Then, wisely, she encouraged her sons by explaining how they would each have to help her with the family responsibilities. "Somehow, we'll make it because we're going to stick together and work together," Kim told them, "The four of us are a team now. We've got to behave like one."

Several months later, Kim looked up from her computer, heard the low hum of the vacuum cleaner and smiled. The previous year had been painful. After her husband left her alone with their three sons, things had been rocky. But now, Kim can recall the change that came over their young faces. "It was miraculous. One moment I was staring into the faces of three hopeless, broken boys. The next, they were ready to fight the odds and start trying again." Kim credits this change in attitude to a single element: interdependence.

Once Kim had communicated to her kids the need to work as a team, her boys felt more empowered to do just that. Kim instinctively recognized that allowing her children to sit idly and amass feelings of anger, guilt, and frustration did nothing to help heal their wounds. Her sons had to believe that their efforts could make a difference. As soon as

Kim was able to transfer this key principle of family members living interdependently—depending on one another for the overall success of the family—the children felt a weight lifted off their shoulders. Young as they were, Kim's boys could help the ones they loved most.

Unlike Kim who realized early on that working together brings profit for the entire family, Tina believed the opposite. Several years after her divorce, she still looked haggard and depressed. Her belief was that her children had suffered enough already and she wasn't about to add to their burden by asking them to help her. So Tina cleaned, cooked, and maintained the yard, and her children continued to throw harsh, rebellious jibes at her: "It's your fault we don't have more money." "Why can't you take us now?" "Wait until I tell Dad you said no!"

Perhaps years from now Tina will realize her efforts to lessen the stress in her home are doing just the opposite, that her home is a time bomb waiting to explode. Relieving young people of responsibilities doesn't create the sense of emotional well-being essential to healthy family life. It does the reverse. Allowing kids to stew in their own selfishness and pampering them because a parent feels guilty only makes a difficult situation worse.

Think back to when you were a child. Can you recall being asked to help around the house? Maybe your job was taking out the trash or feeding and watering the pets. Whatever the task, you had a part in making your family run more smoothly. Hopefully, your parent(s) imparted this sense of community to you as a youngster. Even if they didn't, you probably already knew your contributions made a difference.

Unfortunately, many single moms identify the emotional pain in their kids as something they directly (or indirectly) caused. In one sense, this is true. However, even two-parent families have times of disagreement, tension, and unresolved issues. But you can bet that chores still get done regardless. So when family life gets tough, everyone has to pitch in and put forth some effort. It is essential that you and your children realize you're all integral parts of the family. No matter how the family unit is identified (single- or two-parent) every family must function as its own entity.

As you learn to communicate this sense of unity (and dependence upon one another) as Kim did, your entire family will gain a feeling of security. You will also gain a more complete sense of family identity. You'll notice individual self-worth will flourish too. Families were instituted by God. He has established home life as the place for maturity to blossom and grow. When we look to his Word and follow his principles, our family life will be brought to fruition in ways we never dreamed possible. Try out a few of the ideas described below to spark that all important interdependent feeling in your own family; you'll soon notice a blessed change.

Ideas for Strengthening Your Family Identity

• **Design a chore list.** Break down the jobs into daily, weekly, monthly, and occasional sections. Assign each family member their own chores (respective of age and ability). Chart this information on a blank calendar. Everyone in the family should have daily chores such as making his or her own bed, caring for a pet, tidying the bedroom. Create a weekly chart by dividing all cleaning responsibilities for each week. Everyone takes a section for the week and completes the work. Rotate this list monthly. For the monthly and occasional tasks, be more flexible. Complete these tasks on weekends or inclement weather days.

Karissa divided the household chores and yard work between her son, her daughter, and herself. She wrote these lists on a large calendar she displays on her refrigerator. Now, no one has the excuse of forgetting what chores they are supposed to do.

• **Instill the importance of working together like teammates.** The first Saturday in May, Loretta treated her children to a minor league baseball game. After the game, they went to a pizza parlor for dinner. As they ate, Loretta commented on how well the winning team played together. Her son Adam enthusiastically pointed out how important teamwork was to winning a game. Pleased with her son's insights, Loretta drew parallels between teamwork on the field and in the home.

She reminded him that sports teams would not succeed if each teammate weren't willing to set aside his own interests in favor of the team's overall well-being. You too can encourage your children to think about how their actions will affect the rest of the family.

- **Pray together over family issues.** Be it at the dinner table or around the bed, make praying with your children a priority. Share your own needs and ask them what things you can specifically pray for them about. Then call upon your Heavenly Father together. Take turns praying aloud. Keep a journal of prayer requests and answers as a testimony of God's continual provision. Memorize scripture promises together and practice reciting them.

Marge did this when she challenged her girls to memorize an entire chapter of Scripture before school started in the fall. Right after dinner cleanup, Marge opened her Bible and the girls took turns reciting their passages. Within six weeks, Marge and her children had completely committed the entire chapter to memory. Marge marveled at how her girls' prayers began to change as they recalled certain promises found in their memory verses and incorporated them into their prayers of faith.

- **Attend church and church functions as a family.** Surround your family with those of like belief and influence. Bring your children into a body of believers who will accept, love, and nurture them. Get involved in the fun extras of church fellowship, such as kid's clubs, choirs, vacation bible schools, drama, and missions.

For example, when Bethany's church put out a call for someone to host the junior high youth group in his or her home, she volunteered. She opened her home every other Sunday evening to the junior high students and their club leaders. She was thrilled to see so many young people gathering together on a regular basis for fun and fellowship. Best of all, her own children were right in the middle of the action.

• **Be hospitable to the needy.** At the end of each season, Candace and her children go through their clothes and toys. They gather up clothing that's too small and toys that aren't of interest. Candace takes these items to the women's crisis shelter in her town.

Another idea is to search out those who need some extra attention or assistance. It doesn't cost much to spend a few hours cleaning a yard for an elderly neighbor or making a meal for a family with a new baby. Enlist the entire family to help serve in these important ways.

• **Encourage your children to develop their spiritual gifts.** Help children discover how God uniquely fashioned them. Study the Scriptures and discuss various gifts. These gifts include wisdom, faith, healing, discernment, serving, teaching, mercy, giving, administration, and many others (Rom. 2:3–8; 1 Cor. 12:7–11). Be alert to ways each family member naturally gravitates toward using certain gifts in daily living.

Patty Ann also listed the fruit of the Spirit (Gal. 5:22–23) individually on 3 x 5 index cards. She handed one card to each of her children. They were to observe their siblings and write a notation each time they recognized the virtue specified on their card being lived out. By the end of the week, each child had become more sensitive to what it means to live by the Spirit.

• **Don't be afraid to say no.** Pressures to participate in activities from school, family, friends, and church can threaten to extinguish quality family life. If necessary, limit the number of extra-curricular functions. Try to find activities more than one family member can participate in.

Allison laid down the law as she insisted that her four children choose only one extracurricular activity. She explained that with mid-week club meetings at their church and piano lessons on Friday, their schedule and hers could only accommodate one other choice. That summer, all four kids decided to play community softball which held Allison's driving time to a tolerable level.

• **Have fun together.** Set aside times for simply having fun. Discover interesting local sites for picnics, Rollerblading, ice-skating, and biking.

On hot summer evenings, take advantage of free concerts. Learn to relax together.

Every Thursday, Barb's kids scoured the evening newspaper for the weekend's special events. In rotation, Barb allowed her children to select one free local event to attend during the upcoming weekend. Her kids loved being given a choice, and the variety of events they chose kept them from getting bored.

• **Love unconditionally.** Foster a spirit of camaraderie and oneness by loving as Christ did and forgiving as Christ commanded. Remember, interdependence is more than just activity, it's an attitude. It's recognizing how much we really need each other and then communicating this to those we love. Encourage your family to depend on God, and upon each other.

Rachel left little notes of affirmation tucked under her children's pillows at night. On these notes, Rachel would sometimes write an instruction or a request, too. She would suggest that the note's recipient get back out of bed and go hug a sibling. Or, Rachel might ask her child to be praying for his brother or sister if either was facing a special situation the following day.

Allow God the opportunity to knit your family together with the bond of his enduring love.

4

Building Bridges:

Communicating with

Uncooperative People

*T*hirty-nine-year-old Melissa Carver jumped in her seat when she heard the child's cry from somewhere behind her in the movie theater. She thought she was long past reacting like a scared rabbit every time she heard a child cry. Still feeling a bit panicky, Melissa excused herself and went out to the concession stand to purchase something to drink. Diversion, that's what some psychologist would call her habit. Melissa laughed. She didn't care what anyone said. An ice cold soda always went a long way toward soothing her jangled nerves.

Back in her seat and contentedly sipping her Coke, Melissa's thoughts strayed from the movie's plot to somewhere back in time. Four years back, to be precise. After Jake had left, she learned a lot about loneliness, anger, resentment, and fear. She would have given anything for the earth to open up and swallow her. But it hadn't, and now she was glad. The sun had kept coming up and she had been forced to move forward.

Now she was a bit worse for the wear, perhaps, but stronger. She really was satisfied with her life. Jess and Nancy were doing well in their sixth and eighth grade classes. Even Brenton was thriving on his new regimen. From where she sat, the future looked pretty good. But, Melissa sobered, she never wanted to forget where she'd come from, that dark place God had delivered her from.

From the moment Melissa brought Brenton, her youngest child, home from the hospital, he cried, deeply and soulfully. Jake laughingly called their son the home's resident noisemaker. But Melissa sensed something was truly wrong with him.

She was right. After a series of medical consultations, tests, and x-rays, Melissa and Jake were told that Brenton had several medical problems, not the least of which was a digestive disorder that caused the little guy no end of pain and discomfort. In time and with the right medical care, Brenton should get better, the doctor assured them. Still, he cautioned, it would take years for his small body to develop, mature, and recover. Surgery was an absolute given. Lifelong medical treatments were a very real possibility.

Ill equipped to cope with this news, Melissa instinctively turned her full attention on seeing to it that Brenton got the best care available. They endured numerous surgeries. Recovery time, both in the hospital and at home, kept Melissa in a permanent state of readiness. Between caring for Brenton and their other two children, Jake and Melissa spent little time alone together. Their priority was to do what was best for Brenton. Whenever she and Jake got into an argument over burgeoning medical bills, she reminded Jake that they didn't have a choice. Jake disagreed.

As Brenton's condition stabilized and Melissa's hectic schedule became less demanding, she started looking forward to a more normal family life. After all, she and Jake had just weathered the worst, so they could now relish some long awaited time for the two of them. Longing for some adult intimacy, Melissa turned to Jake for companionship. But she discovered he had already turned to someone else.

Melissa can still vividly picture the moment of truth. Jake driving into the garage. Jake walking in the back door. Jake quietly closing the door of their bedroom. Jake nudging her gently to see if she was still awake. Then, Jake telling her he wanted a divorce. It was that simple. No dramatic scenes, no shouting. No tears shed. Just a chilling numbness.

Within three months, they were divorced. Melissa felt dumbfounded that such a major life change could happen so quickly. She puzzled at other single moms who shared with her the difficulties of their own divorce proceedings. She could relate to the pain, but Jake was great about monthly child support, the house, and the kids.

Melissa's adjustment to single parenting was tough. She was grateful for Jake's amiable attitude. He went to great lengths to make certain she and the kids were okay.

Then Jessica, the future Mrs. Jake Carver, entered their lives. Melissa knew this wasn't simply the newest in a long line of casual girlfriends Jake had been involved with since the birth of their son Brenton. Jake was serious about Jessica. Looking back, Melissa could almost pinpoint the day and hour Jake changed his tune toward her and the kids. Where he had shown positive qualities, the influence of Jessica now had him challenging Melissa's decisions, undermining her efforts in raising their children, and sabotaging her financial resources.

Left without a father, Melissa's children lost every tiny measure of security. Melissa and Jake's divorce became a war zone. Melissa dreaded the days when Jake came to pick up the kids. She hid inside the house and shooed the kids outside as soon as she saw his car drive up. She even went so far as to lock herself in the bathroom whenever she suspected Jake might come inside to help the kids unload their bags. Tired of all the conflict and intimidation, Melissa knew she had to take some kind of action. The anticipation and trepidation of another confrontation was killing her. She had no choice but to try something, anything.

"I need to learn how to communicate with Jake without fighting," she said. "I just don't know if it's possible anymore. We've both fallen into such a vicious cycle of me asking and him refusing, me demanding and him threatening. So, if talking doesn't cut it, what are my options? How can I approach someone who's totally unapproachable?"

After many trials and errors, Melissa did learn how to communicate with Jake. She initially tried the hit-and-miss method. Melissa would try one way. If it worked, good. If not, she'd try something else. Over the next twelve months, Melissa became quite adept at working through visitation changes, medical alterations, and holiday planning challenges. Melissa learned what pushed Jake's buttons, and she avoided those touchy areas. Most importantly, Melissa removed herself from the battle lines and refused to be drawn into a fight. Her only goal was to develop and maintain a relationship with Jake that would ensure protection and provision for her children. Melissa's methods of communication were not complicated. She discovered time-tested ways to speak without becoming angry, make requests without being demanding, and communicate with integrity to those lacking it.

The lessons Melissa learned through her trial and error with Jake carried over to other parts of her life. She became more confident in her work environment. She handled uncomfortable requests from associates and friends with resolve and tact. Melissa's entire social structure was enhanced by what she learned.

Your life, like Melissa's, can change for the better, too. Maybe you're in a similar situation and you can't imagine a conversation with your ex-spouse that doesn't end in threats and angry words. Or, perhaps your relationship with your former spouse is already acceptable. Whatever scenario you see yourself in, there is always room for improvement. Obviously, divorce wasn't a part of your plans. It wasn't part of Melissa's either. But now that you've entered the unique world of single parenting, you can effectively work through the nitty-gritties of child rearing in a productive and positive manner. The following are simple suggestions for improving the lines of communication with uncooperative individuals in your life.

Simple Steps to Better Communication

• **Develop realistic expectations.** When Tuesday softball games are scheduled for your child's team and your ex-spouse doesn't show up, don't feign shock. Whenever a spouse abandons the family, it is already clear he views his own needs as top priority. The very act of leaving is perhaps the most selfish of all. Thus, all succeeding acts of neglect simply reinforce this initial decision. Purpose in your mind to expect nothing. If your ex-spouse does make an occasional altruistic gesture, be grateful. But don't anticipate overnight turnabouts.

Amanda prepped herself prior to every one of Matt's soccer games. She breathed a silent prayer for patience and asked God for grace. If Ron did show up for Matt's game, great. If not, God still gave Amanda the peace of mind she needed to cope with her ex-husband's misguided priorities.

• **Be open-minded and flexible.** Single parenting can throw the custodial parent off balance at times. Just when life seems to be temporarily flat-lining, an unexpected emergency can leave a parent's mind and emotions gasping for relief. Instead of gathering reinforcements in an effort to do battle with the unexpected or uncontrollable, purpose to develop a more flexible attitude in response to life. Turn to God before the tragedy occurs, in the midst of suffering, and after the winds of adversity have calmed.

• **Plan your words in advance.** Busy adults make use of daily planners to map out upcoming events as a way to protect against schedule overload. Planning conversations with an ex-spouse should be handled with the same forethought. Prioritize your needs as well as your children's. Don't overwhelm your ex-spouse with too many expectations at one meeting. Explain your requests and provide the needed information in written form if possible. Keep it simple. Set reasonable timetables for your ex-spouse to consider what you've shared.

For example, Amy wrote her daughter Ashley's newest schedule out for her ex-husband, Thad. They needed to share in transporting Ashley to rehab over the next eight weeks. Amy divided the appointments evenly and offered to take either alternative schedule. Thad appreciated Amy's willingness to be flexible and he ended up chauffeuring their daughter to her rehab sessions the majority of the eight weeks.

- **Pray that God will guide your ex-spouse's decisions.** Spend time daily going over your prayer needs. As you pray, beseech God to intervene in your ex-spouse's mind and heart to the benefit of your children (rather than your own). Keep in mind that your ultimate goal is to develop a relationship which glorifies God and is workable for the sake of your children.

Diane keeps a special prayer journal for those interactions between her and her ex-husband. Prior to any major request or decision, Diane enters a recording of the situation. Over the years, this journal has brought more encouragement to Diane than she ever expected. She sometimes thinks that God simply delights in presenting an obstacle, just so he can demonstrate to Diane how he is able to solve it.

- **Write letters instead of communicating in person or by telephone.** When marriages break up, some divorced adults can continue to converse without animosity; others cannot or will not. Taking pen in hand is perhaps one of the most effective methods to employ when making an alteration in custody, discussing a new procedure in medical treatments, or addressing any number of complicated changes. It's possible to write a letter with simple clarity, devoid of negative emotions, so the recipient will read it and digest its contents in a way that is comfortable to him. As you share your options, be positive and not blaming. Be assertive, not aggressive. Offer workable solutions and be willing to adapt. Ask for a response by a given date. Withhold the urge to call and discuss the matter before the specified day. In the interim, pray for God's hand to be on the situation and relax in that knowledge.

Julie makes copies of all her children's medical records and sends them to her ex-husband, Jon. Since he is responsible for paying the children's medical expenses, Julie feels it's best for Jon to see the doctor's findings and receipts. Julie has noticed Jon doesn't fight against paying the bills once he's had the opportunity to review them.

• **Offer to bring in an objective third party.** Some circumstances are too heated or too painful for an estranged couple to deal with on their own. In these cases, try bringing in an impartial outsider as a mediator. Ask your former husband to select a person of his own choosing. When you evidence a willingness to meet with your ex-spouse's choice of mediator and adopt an attitude of genuine humility, he's more likely to be flexible, especially if he's confident you're interested primarily in what's best for your children, not in your own personal gain. The key is being willing to let go of any perceived "power" you hold over an ex-husband.

Tired of fighting, Danita left the choice of a counselor up to her ex-spouse, Randy. For three months, they'd argued over petty differences and hadn't resolved any of the decisions which faced them. Danita agreed to meet with Randy at a time convenient to them both. Surprisingly, the counselor was impartial and many of their decisions were resolved within a few sessions.

• **Encourage your children to forgive.** Kathy never thought she'd live to see the day when she could actually enter into a conversation with Jim without feeling burning resentment toward him. But that was before Kathy's dad, Colin, was dying of cancer. Colin told her how he had regretted living all those years in stoic, silent anger toward his own ex-wife, Kathy's mom. As Kathy saw her father wasting away, she also saw him spending his last days on earth full of regret over his past resentment and unforgiveness. She resolved to stop that legacy then and there. Kathy couldn't bear to think her current attitudes could be the cause of her own children's inability to love and forgive in the future.

Children will find it almost impossible to forgive their absent parent if they observe the custodial parent harboring bitterness and anger. As children see their custodial parent working through the long, difficult process of forgiveness, they too, will have a model for their own life. Every person, divorced or not, will be given many opportunities to put into practice the process of lasting forgiveness. What better place to begin than in the home? You and your children will never live to regret embracing mercy and love over retribution and resentment.

5

Finding Fulfillment:

Spreading Your Horizons

as a Single Mom

Maggie rushed through her makeup and hair styling routine in order to make it to her class on time. Then the phone rang. Picking up the receiver, Maggie dropped her can of hair spray when she recognized her ex-husband's voice on the other end. She needn't have bothered listening any further. She knew why Jack was calling—to cancel, again. Hanging up the phone, she hurriedly dialed her friend Kendra's number. Please be home, she prayed. Maggie only waited two rings before her prayer was answered.

"Kendra, it's me, Maggie. Listen, Jack was supposed to pick up the kids for the morning and he just called to cancel. Is your offer still open?"

"Bring them right over. You'll still have time to make your class if you hurry."

"Thanks, Kendra. You're a lifesaver. See you in a few minutes. Kristen, Jeremy, get your coats and bags. We're leaving now!"

"But Mom, I thought Dad was supposed to pick us up!" protested Kristen.

"He was, but plans have changed and you're going to Kendra's instead," Maggie hurriedly explained.

"I don't want to go over there again. Kendra's kids are too little to play with us. Anyway, their dog always jumps on me."

"I know this isn't what you had in mind for a fun Saturday; but this class is important to me. Remember last fall how we talked about me going back to school?"

"Yeah, Mom. But going to Kendra's every week wasn't part of the deal."

"Come on, kids. Into the car," Maggie urged.

Later, Maggie glanced down at the speedometer and pulled her foot slightly away from the accelerator. If she could miss those early morning trains that sometimes blocked the route to her class, she'd still be on time. Slow down. Relax, she told herself. Going to school was supposed to be a good thing.

Sitting in the classroom minutes later, Maggie breathed a sigh of contented relief. Now she could take off her Mommy hat and her Jack's ex-wife hat. Here she was just Maggie, another adult heading back to college for some classes. She smiled. There was a part of her that relished the anonymity of it all. No one here knew what she'd been through. Week after week, this was the one place where she really felt like she was starting over and building a new life for herself and the kids. She loved it.

As her instructor delved into his lesson, Maggie took diligent notes. Next week was her third exam, she reminded herself. She'd need to take time each night this week for an hour of study. The kids and she'd be working around the table together. They'd get a kick out of that. Now if she could only convince Jack that she wasn't neglecting the children by going back to college. He'd promised to support them financially. Still, this wasn't just about making more money. She needed to find a place for herself, somewhere she could see herself heading in the next five years or so. Completing her degree would afford her more options, too. What amazed her was how energized she felt these days. Just getting out a few hours a week had given her a whole new sense of adventure. It also rebirthed her hope in the future. Sometimes change was good.

Taking on the role of a single mom means having to carve out some time for yourself. In order to survive the emotional strains of raising children alone, you have to give yourself some well defined space as well as opportunities for personal and social growth. Taking time for your own needs can help ease what many singles term "those lonely Saturdays when I ain't got nobody" syndrome—that sad, forlorn feeling you get whenever you see "intact" families together, and having fun.

It's no surprise to single moms like Maggie that weekends tend to be among the toughest times emotionally. After a long week of juggling kids' schedules and meeting your own responsibilities, single parents desperately need the weekend to rejuvenate and relax. Often, however, the weekends become a time of dissatisfaction and loneliness.

As Maggie confided, "I suddenly woke up one day about a year and a half after my divorce and realized how desperately bored I was with me. Since I was no longer married, I also felt very alone. Finally, I decided I needed some intellectual stimulation, something to keep my mind occupied. School seemed like the perfect choice. It's also given me a real boost in self-confidence. Not that it isn't sometimes a chore to get there," she admitted. "But once I walk through the door and sit down, I relax and realize there's a whole world out there. Maybe the best part is, I'm finding I can still be a part of it."

Society, too, does its own class act of alienating single adults with kids (often by omission). The weekends, advertisers purport, are perfect for romantic getaways. What emotional message does that evoke in the single man or woman? Or take sporting events where the norm is for fathers and sons to be together. How does a single mom compensate? Should she just pretend not to notice? You can bet her son is painfully aware that Dad is missing.

Single mom Kari recalls early Saturday morning soccer practices with a grimace: "Those practices were a particular sore point with me because the coach would invite all the fathers and sons out for a late breakfast after practice each week. But he never included us mothers and our sons. I know how alienated my son, Aaron, felt. But what could I do? I realize the coach probably wasn't comfortable inviting single mothers. But it still hurt. We never really resolved the problem either."

The loss of normal weekday routines when schedules become more casual or even nonexistent can also contribute to weekend woes. As soon as everyone wakes up on Saturday morning, there's an expectancy to have big fun simply because it's the weekend. So if the head of the family hasn't made exciting plans, then disappointment and irritation often surface.

Emily, the mother of two preteen sons, was awakened every Saturday morning with the question, "What are we going to do today?" After months of frustration on both sides, she now takes her sons over to her parents' house two Saturdays a month for a big breakfast. Then Emily's dad and the boys work on a carpentry project. On opposite weeks, she treats her sons to a sporting event. Emily says, "Alternating visiting at my folks' house and going out helps keep the cost down without sacrificing the fun."

So how does a single mom whose feeling either stressed or alone and lonely start the process of finding relief and inner satisfaction for herself?

Assess your resources. Ask yourself, what funds are available? Do you have the budgeting savvy to rework your finances to include some money for leisure activities? Or is your budget so tight that even small amounts are impossible? Once you determine what your financial resources are, you will find yourself narrowing down initial options based solely on the cost.

Then, consider the time element. Do you have extra time available for a venture every Saturday or Sunday? Or does your schedule only permit outings twice monthly? Don't forget your children's commitments either. The goal is to build into your own life interesting, challenging, and life-giving experiences without sacrificing your children's activities.

Once you determine your financial resources and the flexibility of your schedule, consider your own interests. Are there hobbies you've always wanted to try but never have? Are you interested in either completing or continuing work towards a degree? What about service opportunities stemming from your local church or a volunteer agency? Is your greatest need simply more time out socially? Then tailor your plan according to your specific needs and long-term goals.

Finally, set your desires and goals down on paper. Don't be afraid to dream. God knows our innermost needs and desires before we even recognize them ourselves. Enlist his help through prayer. Make a plan to start meeting your goals within six to eight weeks, if possible. Check into the details, count the costs, set aside funds, and work toward making your dreams a reality. Never forget that a little planning today makes a big difference tomorrow.

Plan Today for Tomorrow

• **Set a reasonable time schedule.** Eliminate unnecessary weekend time-wasting clutter like house cleaning and grocery shopping. Pick one weekday to grocery shop and break down cleaning to single, daily chores. Break big tasks into smaller pieces.

Joyce loved to cook. She would lug home numerous gourmet cook books each time she and her children visited their local library. On Thursday, Joyce planned her next gourmet meal. On Friday, she shopped. On Saturday morning, she got up early and spent the morning experimenting in the kitchen.

• **Make a list of your long- and short-term personal achievement goals.** Write down in detail the steps required to reach each goal. Ask questions, such as, What do I want to have accomplished five years from now? What obstacles make reaching that goal seem impossible? What steps can I take this week or this month to remove the obstacles?

• **Choose one activity from both your long- and short-term goals and start gathering pertinent information for both tasks.** Begin with your short-term goal. Call for costs and sign-up dates. Then make arrangements for the children. Enlist the help of family and friends. Take turns baby-sitting with other single moms. For example, Marlene's kickboxing classes are held from 6:00 to 8:00 P.M., Monday, Wednesday, and Friday. Her neighbor, Peg, comes over during those hours to watch Marlene's baby boy, Michael. In exchange, Marlene cleans Peg's house weekly and irons for her, too.

Next, research your long-term goal and make a point of reviewing this goal sheet monthly to reevaluate. Be flexible. Your goals may change drastically with time.

Because of her love for animals, Renee had always wanted to work in veterinarian's office. She couldn't think of a better job than to assist injured animals. One class at a time, Renee is working toward her dream. If she stays on schedule, she'll have completed her training within eighteen months.

• **Enjoy some well-earned time for yourself.** Brenda takes their family dog on a long walk after dinner each evening. She relishes the solitude and enjoys the quiet time to gather her thoughts. After about an hour, Brenda returns home with a healthy flush on her cheeks and a renewed sense of energy.

Refuse to feel guilty for wanting and needing some personal time away from your children. You'll come back refreshed, revitalized, and with more to give after you've had a breather. Strive for balance in every area. Let your children learn from an early age that there is a time for rest and a time for work. You've shown them how to work; now show them how to play.

Suggested Activities and Opportunities

- **Attend the symphony or pop concerts** (local groups often give free concerts at parks during summer months).
- **Attend theater productions** (high school and community college plays often have low cost tickets).
- **Visit art museums.**
- **Patronize libraries** (borrow instructional videos, movies, books on hobbies).
- **Visit recreational parks** (sign up for nature walks and exploration tours, walk, run, bike, skate, go to an observatory).
- **Attend sporting events** (buy season tickets to your favorite team, join a softball league, go to the gym to swim or work out, learn tap dancing).
- **Pursue higher education** (finish high school or college, take adult education classes for credit or for fun, develop new skills through community education courses).
- **Volunteer** (consider the local crisis pregnancy center, soup kitchens for the homeless, 4-H clubs, or Big Brother/Big Sister organizations).
- **Participate in church ministries and/or social functions** (start singing in the choir, lead Children's Worship, teach a Sunday School class, join the drama team).

6

Thinking Critically:

Encouraging Kids to Discern

S itting in the lunch room cafeteria, thirteen-year-old Ross and his friend Eric were talking about an invitation both received from a fellow classmate.

"Did you decide if you're going or not?" asked Eric.

"I'm not sure yet . . . " replied Ross.

"What do you mean? Didn't Ben's mom say it was all right if we went to the concert with them on Saturday?" asked Eric in disbelief.

"Yeah, but that's a death metal band Ben's going to see," Ross answered. "I don't think my mom would want me to go."

"I can't believe you. What's the problem? Ben's our friend. He even goes to the same church as us. If his mom said it's okay, then why are you holding back?"

"I don't know. Something just doesn't seem right about it."

"Well, I'm going. I wouldn't miss it. See ya, Ross."

Maybe Eric is right, Ross thought. Maybe I am crazy.

If Ross' mother had been able to listen in on this conversation between her son and his friend, no doubt she would have been proud. But unfortunately being proud of her son isn't enough to ensure he'll make the right decision next time around. Obviously, his mom has made a positive impact on his decision-making processes already. But Ross continues to wonder whether he's made the right decision. Why? Because Ross hasn't been taught one of the most valuable lessons a parent can pass onto their children—how to think critically. If Ross had been coached at home on how to think through decisions with more intellectual skill, he would have been able to make his choice with confidence. Ross would not only have known why his mom wouldn't like him going to a death metal concert, he would have been able to think through the process for himself and the convictions would have been his own.

As adults, we are wizened to the schemes of advertisers who tell us exactly what they think we want to hear. Justifiably, we are wary and even go so far as to protect our children from as many sources of untruth as possible. Our children face many scoffers and constant opposition to the values we attempt to instill in them. Wouldn't it be wise to instruct our children in the art of critical thinking in the same manner as we teach basics like reading, writing, and arithmetic?

Without a doubt, in the average neighborhood kids are going to observe inappropriate and even illegal behavior. The reasoning that says, "Since everybody is doing it, it must be OK" must be dealt with. Perhaps they'll hear that premarital sex really isn't that much of a risk because of the widespread availability of condoms, with a nice legal abortion available as a last resort. Subtle, potentially volatile messages are reinforced week after week, and our children need to know how to think through and resolve conflicting messages.

Neighborhoods aren't the only place where kids pick up thinly veiled untruths. In our media blitzed society, children receive messages from the radio, television, the Internet, books, the work place, school, and even some churches. Protecting and sheltering are fine aspirations. But in today's culture, parents need to prepare and practice the art of critical thinking necessary for their children's intellectual, emotional, and spiritual survival.

The process of critical thinking is simple. It includes:

1. observation
2. contemplation
3. deduction/resolution.

We encourage our kids to observe by asking questions after we've read a book together. We spark the contemplation process by posing questions which force them to think about the effects of certain behaviors or specific attitudes. We challenge our kids' deductive abilities by asking them what they believe is the right course to follow and why.

1. Observation. Jenny watched a PBS special on early civilizations. Great program, excellent material, except for one questionable part discussing the origins of man. While the show was on, Jenny's mom heard bits and pieces of the program from the kitchen where she was working. Alerted by some fallacies, she decided to discuss the program at dinner.

2. Contemplation. At the supper table, Jenny and her mom talked about the theories espoused in the show. Jenny agreed that yes, she was puzzled about some aspects of the program. But she didn't think any further about it. Mom, on the other hand, asked Jenny to observe what was expressed as fact. Once Jenny identified the area purported as fact, her mom asked her to think through what knowledge she already had and where she got her information from.

3. Deduction/resolution. After thinking about this problem for a few moments, Jenny was then able to make a more definite mental decision deducing that what she heard was not entirely correct, and she filed this information away.

Jenny's mom may not know it, but she has begun teaching her daughter not to assume every statement stemming from a supposed authority is accurate. She has also planted the seed for Jenny to begin critically thinking about the information she gathers. As Jenny puts this process into practice, she will find it becomes natural—a habit. Jenny is not encouraged to be a rebel or to be belligerent. She is, however, going to be more sensitive to error and more ready to process the messages that come her way.

For most families, the process of critical thinking already occurs unknowingly. It is instinctive for parents to teach and instruct children in the truth. If we pause for a moment and reflect, we might be surprised how many critical thinking exercises we currently practice. For those who aren't sure how to begin spurring this process in their kids' lives, take a look at the following ideas.

Ways to Teach Your Child Critical Thinking Skills

• **Ask questions.** Try posing verbal math problems which activate and energize the mind. Then ask your child to explain the process they went through to obtain the answer. During stops at their grocery store, Bonnie asked her children to do quick add-ups of various grocery store items. If they were able to correctly add the items in under a minute, Bonnie allowed them one treat of their choice.

• **Watch television and video programs together.** View television programs and videotapes, or play video games together and discuss the behavior, attitudes, and resulting consequences with your children by asking open-ended questions. Judy and her children spent every Friday night watching videos they borrowed from their library. She allowed them the privilege of staying up late on Friday in exchange for five minutes of discussion after each movie. Judy ended up learning as much about her children as her children did from formulating responses to Judy's questions.

• **Read aloud as a family.** Read books aloud and talk about the characters. What characters did your children like best and sympathize with most? Why were they attracted to these particular people? What did these specific persons do which was right or wrong? For example, Maddie asked her children to tell her one thing they learned from the story she read to them each night. Maddie never knew what to expect. Lessons ranged from hilarious to horrifying.

• **Watch commercials.** Take advantage of those insidious commercial breaks. Sitting with pen and pencil, listen actively to commercials and write down as many misleading statements as you can detect in each ad. Each statement must be backed up by explanations sharing why the statement was misleading. *Note:* the subject content of early afternoon and Saturday morning commercials is generally less offensive to young minds.

Haley gave each of her children a cereal box. She asked them to carefully read the advertising found on it. After about five minutes, they all discussed the promises and whether or not each one was legitimate.

• **Take advantage of computer technology.** Borrow or buy computer programs aimed at developing critical thinking skills using memory, problem solving, and creativity. Jodi gets shareware computer software for her kids to try at home. She then purchases only those programs her kids find particularly interesting.

• **Use educational resource materials.** During the summer months, Ruth offers to pay her children play money for every five pages they complete in educational workbooks. After they've accumulated fifty play dollars in their account, Ruth takes them to their local dollar store where they can shop with five real dollars. You can do the same. A good resource for the workbooks is Critical Thinking Press & Software which incorporates figures, words, pictures, and much more to sharpen the thinking skills of kids of all ages. This publisher offers numerous types of books stimulating the thinking skills in areas such as language arts, mathematics, science, social studies, and ethics. For more information, call 1-800-458-4849.

• **Use family life to provoke thinking.** Take advantage of real life family dilemmas—sibling struggles, defying authority, selfish attitudes—to work through using the critical thinking process. For example, Shirley plays *Wheel of Fortune* every time her kids fall into a pattern of negative behavior or attitudes. She writes a biblical principle on a piece of paper and asks each child in turn to provide a letter. They continue calling out letters until one of the children guesses the correct principle. The winner gets to decide on dessert for that day.

In short, invest the time and energy required to initiate and enhance your children's critical thinking skills. Every effort extended toward that end, will reap untold benefits throughout the lives of every child.

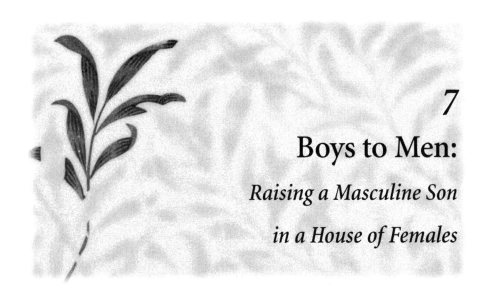

7

Boys to Men:

Raising a Masculine Son
in a House of Females

*E*laine sat thumping her fingers on the table next to the telephone. Should she or shouldn't she? Elaine debated calling her mom to cry on her shoulder about Scott for the umpteenth time that month. For a kid who was only fifteen years old, Scott had done more to give her gray hair than anyone deserved. Not stopping to consider further, Elaine dialed her mom's telephone number. She was relieved when her mom picked up the phone on the first ring.

"Oh, Mom, what am I going to do about Scott?" moaned Elaine.

"What are you talking about, Honey?" her mom asked. Inwardly, Elaine's mom dreaded hearing about her grandson's latest antics. Scott had been a complacent child before Elaine and Matt got the divorce. She chuckled.

"Mom! Are you listening to me?" cried Elaine impatiently.

"Yes, Elaine, I hear you. I was just thinking about how Scott used to be so . . . so . . ."

"Go ahead, Mom. Say it," interrupted Elaine, "Scott used to be such a nice kid and now he's a terror."

"Elaine, I was thinking no such thing. Scott is . . . well . . . spirited. And he's the only boy you have. You can hardly compare him with Jamie or Ashley."

"Don't I know it!" Elaine said. "But this time he's gone too far."

"What exactly did he do?"

"Mom, he went out and got his nose and his eyebrow pierced. Seems a friend from school works at the mall and she did it for him . . . without my consent. I can't even bear to think about how Matt's going to respond when he sees Scott this weekend," Elaine said with obvious despair in her voice.

"Elaine, listen to me. Scott may look a little funny to you and me, but it's not the end of the world, dear."

"Mom, you know Matt. He already thinks I'm making a mama's boy out of Scott. When he sees his only son come out of the house wearing not one, but two stud earrings on his face he's going to explode and I don't want to be anywhere around." Elaine shuddered as she imagined the possibilities.

"Well, I'll be praying . . ."

"Better add fasting to those prayers, Mom. This is serious," Elaine replied.

It will be all right, it will be all right, Elaine chanted to herself later as she prepared for bed. She just had to remain focused. She would not get upset. She would not become angry. She would not yell. So, what was she going to do? Elaine kneaded her aching temples. "Lord," she cried out, "I really think I'm going to explode. I don't know what to do with Scott." When she first divorced, Scott seemed to be handling his dad's absence pretty well. Then he withdrew. They all were depressed. But she thought they'd worked through all that. Now here they were, heading off into yet another fiasco. She knew Scott missed his dad. He sure complained often enough about how he was living with the "Brady ladies." But she was the one with full custody and she was confident that it was for the best. Matt traveled far too much for him to make a stable home for any of the kids.

Maybe it was time she took her brother's advice and started looking for ways for Scott to feel like the man he was growing into. She certainly didn't want him feeling like Matt's replacement either. No, she needed to provide Scott with opportunities that would help him channel his creativity and his energy in positive ways. He needed to know what kind of man God wanted him to become. He also needed to know how much she admired and respected him despite all the foolish things he'd done the last couple of years. "Oh, God," Elaine prayed, "Give me the words and the wisdom to help this son of mine. Help me to communicate to Scott just how valuable he is in your sight and in mine."

While it is true that some divorced fathers have full custody of their children, the majority of single parent homes continue to be headed by the mother. This realization raises the question, "How can I provide the masculine influence needed for my son when he lives with me in a home without a father?"

For some, the answer is not so complicated. The father continues to see his children on a regular and frequent basis. Or, relatives pitch in and arrange consistent extended time with the young, fatherless males in their family. Other boys are blessed by the caring contribution of love and time given by men in their church. Yet another source of male influence can come by way of a close friend or neighbor who sees the need and takes a youngster under his wing.

Still, a large portion of fatherless homes remain just that—fatherless. In the emotional wake of a divorce, separation, or death, single parents like Elaine find themselves wanting and needing to bridge the gap left behind by the absent spouse. But Elaine discovered mothers can fill this gap by way of deliberate, practical planning.

Six weeks later, Elaine looked around the yard with admiration. It worked, she rejoiced. My brother had the right idea all along. Now

Scott's skills are showcased for everyone to see, she thought. Turning to her son, Elaine asked, "That wasn't so bad was it, Scott?"

"Well, I can think of better things I'd rather be doing on a Saturday afternoon. But, yeah, it turned out pretty good," Scott said. "I think Dad will like it, too."

"Oh, I'm sure he will." Elaine removed her gardening gloves. "You know, your dad used to sit around in the evenings just planning different ways to landscape our yard."

"He did?" Scott said with surprise.

"Yes. In fact, I still have some of his sketches up in the attic," Elaine shared, "But your dad never got around to actually making any of those changes he designed. Once he started traveling he got too busy."

"You mean I did something even Dad hasn't done?" Scott asked in disbelief.

"Don't look so surprised. There's a lot of potential inside that brain of yours," Elaine smiled.

"Thanks, Mom," Scott replied, "Well, time for a little relaxation."

"Sounds good to me. How about ordering the four of us some pizza?" Elaine suggested.

"Two larges or two extra-larges?" Scott asked.

"Whatever you think." Elaine watched her son enter the house with an exuberance she hadn't seen for a long while. She had missed that part of Scott's personality. "Thank you, Lord," she prayed, "for showing me how to help Scott. I know there will be more rough times ahead, but today I feel like we just crossed a milestone."

If you're a mom with sons, take a moment to read the suggestions below. You'll find a variety of ways to spark that thing we call "masculinity" in our sons. Each idea has been tried and tested by other single moms and their sons. With caring input, guidance, and consistent prayer, every boy can grow up to successful manhood in Christ.

Ideas for Sparking Masculinity in Your Son

• **Accentuate the positive through storytelling.** Provide short, descriptive scenarios of good character qualities found in boys' magazines. Listen to Christian radio's story hour which often features heroic antics of interest to boys, like the Sugar Creek Gang. Read books together as a family then discuss the roles of key characters. Take advantage of any male heroes you read about and refer these books to your son. Ask probing questions such as, "What would you have done in the character's position?" "Would this choice be honoring to the Lord?" "Why or why not?" "How did your favorite character learn from his mistakes?" "If you could say one thing to [the character], what would it be?"

• **Study your family history.** Look into your family's maternal and paternal past. Highlight the men's contributions, careers, and priorities. Give your son something to build upon. If possible, talk with older, wiser men in the family to get a clearer picture of your family's background and roots. Read old family journals. Peruse photo albums with grandparents. Or take this a step further and create a family tree complete with a short biographical sketch of family members to display. Teach your son about his heritage and to be proud of it.

• **Read historical biographies and autobiographies of godly men.** Take special note of their interpersonal relationships, and of their attitudes toward coworkers, family, and friends in general and toward women in particular. Ask your son what stood out most about each man. Help him to see the obstacles each one overcame to succeed. Challenge your son to develop his own dream and make practical, yet flexible, plans to bring the dream to reality. Be positive in your approach. Maturity breeds its own reality.

Meg takes her son Jason along with her to the library and helps him choose a book. He loves American history and early American folklore. Meg skims the book Jason selects, then makes a habit of discussing the book whenever they are in the car together.

• **Give your son the hands-on tools to succeed.** Be it a hobby, sport, or vocational interest, make every attempt to encourage in practical means. Don't allow your own personal likes and dislikes to limit your son's choices. Provide needed freedom for trial and error—repeatedly. If finances are tight, look for used materials. Also, put out the word for broken equipment so your son can practice modifying and repairing these items at home.

Tim lived and breathed computers. His fascination with computer technology was astounding. Karen did her best to keep Tim excited about his hobby. They subscribed to computer magazines, went to computer shows, and Tim even enrolled in a community college computer class. With his knowledge of computers and his technical skills, he's been able to start his own basic computer helps and troubleshooting business.

• **Let your son contribute at home.** Make him part of the functioning of the household by enlisting his efforts. Encourage a teamwork mentality. Simple chores like taking out the trash, lifting heavy objects, painting trim, and lawn care all increase self-worth. Your son will gain the satisfaction of having accomplished something worthwhile in the process. Let him know you couldn't do it without his help.

Donna's teenage son Evan chafed at being assigned indoor housework, but jumped at the chance to take care of the lawn. So Donna handed over to him the yard work. Now Donna's content to handle the indoor chores while her son handles the outside.

• **Encourage your son to develop leadership skills.** Ask your son to plan an afternoon outing or mini vacation. Have him look at maps and study the shortest route. Let him telephone for the best accommodations and rates. Then compare. Ask him to write out a tentative time schedule and go for it! Be sure to provide him with a total expenditure limit in distance, time, and expense.

Linnette did this with her two sons after receiving a sizable tax return. Both Trevor and Connor worked hard to plan their week away from home. They spent hours speculating, preparing, and anticipating their vacation. Linnette believes her sons enjoyed the planning stage as much as the actual time away from home.

- **Treat your son differently than you do your daughters.** Instill in him the high calling of purity and integrity before God. Explain the importance of being a gentleman and extending courtesy to those he encounters. Share and demonstrate gentlemanly manners such as opening a car door for others and giving up a seat for the elderly or infirm. Provide examples of how Jesus led powerfully yet was acutely sensitive to the needs of others.

Each Sunday, June expects her son, Chad, to play the part of a gentleman. When they arrive at their church, he opens her door for her. He pulls her chair out at the dinner table. Chad has even learned to make polite small talk. In exchange for Chad's willingness to go along with his mother's weekly lesson in proper etiquette, Chad is allowed to use the family car for an extended time period.

- **Give him responsibilities which stretch him.** Provide opportunities for him to develop his gifts and talents. Allow your son to have a pet, start up a home business, or take an elective class. Study the gifts of the Spirit together in the Bible. Point out ways you observe him living out his own talents. Discuss new areas of interest for your son to explore and grow in.

Tanya recognized how much her son Andrew loved children. So with his mom's help, Andrew set up a summer afternoon childcare business in their home. Over the summer, Andrew's reputation for both reliability and fun spread. Andrew ended up with a sizable chunk of money in his bank account and a good name.

- **Have your son keep track of his goals, dreams, and accomplishments in a journal.** Tara recognized her son's need for organization and better long-term planning. She handed him a daily planner and a budget and told him that if he faithfully kept these two tools current for one month, she would increase his savings for that month by thirty percent. Her son now looks for other ways to motivate his mom to continue giving out these perks.

Teach your son the power of prayer. Keep a written account of requests and answers. Introduce him to the Son of God at an early age. Open your heart to your child by exhibiting an attitude of dependence on God for all that you have and hope to become as your son's mother. In every area, affirm him. Tell him of your love, your prayers, and your admiration. Then let God bring his life to maturity.

8

Special Needs Kids:

How to Cope, Things to Consider

Paul slammed the screen door behind him as he stomped up the back steps and into the kitchen. "Mom!" he screamed.

What now? Sharon wondered. Her ten-year-old son had asked for permission to play with the neighborhood boys only a few minutes ago. Surely, nothing could have happened this fast. "Oh, Lord, give me what I need to handle what I know is coming," Sharon silently pleaded.

"Mom! Where are you?" Paul bellowed.

"I'm in the laundry room," Sharon called.

Like a miniature cyclone of unbridled energy, Paul threw back the laundry room door with so much force that it hit the wall and slammed shut—right in Paul's face.

Tensing for the upcoming verbal onslaught, Sharon braced herself. "Paul, how many times have I told you to stop slamming doors? You're going to break the hinges loose one of these days," she reminded sternly.

Undaunted by his mother's reprimand, Paul plunged into his tale. "Mom! Do you know what happened?"

"Tell me," Sharon said resignedly.

"Zack and Jon started making fun of me again. They kept calling me 'spaz-man' and I wasn't doing anything, Mom! Aren't you going to do something?" Paul cried.

Sharon stood with one hand resting on a stack of clean socks and underwear. As she looked into her son's face, she couldn't help but notice the twitching of his eyes and the slight but discernible shaking of his head. What could she say? Paul was different from his friends. If she noticed and was irritated by Paul's tics, not to mention his high strung emotions, she had no doubt his friends had reached their limit with his unusual behavior. She really needed to find some way to help Paul with these problems. But right now, how could she heal Paul's broken spirit?

"Honey, maybe it's not the best thing for you to be hanging around Zack and Jon. Maybe we need to see about inviting over some friends from school. Is there anyone from your class you'd like to invite for the afternoon?" Sharon asked gently.

"*Mom!*" Paul bellowed in exasperation. "I don't *have* any friends at school. You know that!"

Desperately wishing to comfort her son, Sharon blurted out the first feeble idea that occurred to her. "Well, when I'm finished here, we'll go for a ride to the park. How does that sound?"

"Oh, great! Then Zack and Jon will really have something to laugh at me about, me hanging out with my mom." Paul turned his back, threw his glove onto the carpet, and bolted upstairs to his bedroom. Sharon could hear various objects being bumped and thudded noisily around.

Returning to her stack of unfolded clothes, Sharon realized she needed to find some way to help her son. She couldn't avoid the problem any longer. Paul was right. He didn't have any friends. She really couldn't blame the other kids either. Paul not only acted differently, he was emotionally volatile, too. They were probably afraid of how he was going to react. Tomorrow morning, she'd make an appointment with his doctor and not leave that office until she got some definitive answers this time. There had to be some options for Paul and the family.

Six weeks and numerous tests and x-rays later, Sharon sat in the waiting room of a specialist. Sharon felt she was finally getting to the root of Paul's problem. She just knew this neurologist, referred to her by her family doctor, was the one to help her son. Today, she'd get the answers she needed.

However, her hopes were dashed, as he said, "Just try to ignore it. I see this often. If he were my child, I wouldn't let it bother me."

Ignore it? Was he joking?

Sharon left the doctor's office with a prescription, a mild headache, and the determination to find the medical support which her child and family needed in order to cope with their challenges. As she looked back to her early conversations with this physician, inwardly, she thanked him. His insensitive comments were the catalyst she needed to pay more attention to a different expert: herself.

Paul was eventually diagnosed with mild Tourette's Syndrome and Obsessive-Compulsive Disorder. His condition was characterized by various involuntary repetitive tics and obsessions. Sharon likened the frustration of her son's condition to lying awake at night listening to the incessant drip of a faucet and knowing you cannot stop the sound.

It was during this revealing conversation with her son's physician that Sharon realized a simple truth. Doctors are just people. They can be wonderfully helpful in solving medical problems, but they are not infallible. A doctor can no more fully understand the difficult personal struggles in the day-to-day, full-time care giving of a needy child than lay persons can understand the demands which face doctors.

Doctors have read the textbooks, earned the degrees, and filled their waiting rooms to capacity. Their diagnoses are often right on target. The testing is state-of-the-art, but sometimes the most needed prescription —understanding—comes up short.

In time, Sharon found the medical team which offered the support her son required. More importantly, Sharon realized she had more answers than she gave herself credit for. It wasn't her educational background, nor was it the discipline of keeping current with the most recent research developments. Sharon had something no one else did. She had on-the-job training and a mother's intuition. Those tools, combined with prayer and the Holy Spirit's help, gave her sufficient support to successfully rear this fabulous child God had entrusted to her.

Walking to her car that afternoon, Sharon soberly determined she was going to help Paul. She didn't care how long it took or how many different physicians she had to see. He was going to get everything he needed to cope with his problems. Not even the callous indifference of a whole team of physicians was going to stop her.

Sharon's determination was the key to finding help for Paul. Surprisingly, the help she discovered were simple methods she fell upon while searching for the right doctor.

If your family has been blessed with a special needs child like Paul, you'll need all the resources you can find. You'll also need a good support team composed of family, friends, and medical professionals. Listed below are a collection of simple ideas which will help sustain and strengthen your family, offered by expert parents like yourself with real experience. Look these suggestions over and select those ideas which best meet your family's current needs. Reminder: you know your child better than anyone else. Use your God-given motherly intuition to help guide you through these uncharted waters of parenting a special needs child. Remember, God has already been where you're going.

Hints from Parents of Special Needs Children

• **Be educated.** As in all areas of life, increased knowledge and understanding can better prepare you for the road ahead. Research your child's problem area thoroughly by studying books, periodicals, and tapes. Local libraries and the Internet are excellent resource sites. Once you have a clearer idea of the symptoms, side effects, and behavioral challenges, you'll cope more effectively. You'll also learn to utilize strategies appropriately.

Meredith felt overwhelmed when her daughter's teacher revealed his suspicion that LeAnn was dyslexic. Then Meredith was told about a support group. She found practical help as well as encouragement as she got to know other families experiencing the same challenges.

• **Be honest with your child and yourself.** Take time to prepare emotionally for a heart-to-heart discussion with your child. Explain what his illness entails, how it will affect his day-to-day life, and what kind of future he can work toward. Share your understanding of the illness with gentle candor. Your child already senses he is different from other kids his age. Stress the positives as much as you are able.

Annie took her son Chris out to a nearby go-cart track. After spending some time careening around the track, they stopped for ice cream. As they ate, Annie talked with Chris about his cerebral palsy. She had just received word that her son's leg needed to be put in a brace again. In an attempt to offset this setback, Annie told her son they'd stop by the sporting goods store on their way home to pick up several pair of sports socks with Chris' favorite hockey team logo to wear under his brace. He accepted the news with surprising grace.

• **Choose friends with care.** Steer your child toward those playmates whose personalities will best mesh with your child's strengths and weaknesses. Finding the ideal friend who forgives easily, is complementary in temperament, and accepts your child's unique traits may be a challenge. Still, this task is worth the effort. Your child already deems himself different, so it is vital to his self-esteem to spend quality time with age-appropriate friends who accept him unconditionally.

Going over her daughter's Sunday school class list carefully, Becky considered each child and her temperament. As a teacher in her daughter Ellen's class, Becky knew these children well. She paused before each name. Then Becky decided on three girls to invite over for a special tea party. At the party, Becky kept close by as she served refreshments and refills. By afternoon's end, Becky was pleased to discover that Ellen had already formed an attachment with her classmates. Best of all, this attachment seemed mutual.

- **Communicate with family and friends.** Prepare your resources, information, and attitude prior to meeting with family and friends to discuss your child's diagnosis. The manner in which you communicate this important information will affect how your family forms its initial impression and reaction toward your child. Determine to set forth the facts in a simple, easy to understand method. Above all, broach the subject with a positive attitude. In most instances, those you share with will react in like manner.

Justine invited her extended family over for a mid-week dessert party. While they were enjoying their desserts, Justine set up a treasure hunt outside. When the kids were out of ear shot, she shared all she knew about her son Ryan's tumor. She even passed out the information given her by her son's physician. Before everyone left that evening, Justine felt more confident knowing her family was up to speed on Ryan's medical progress.

- **Be proactive, not reactive.** Resist the urge to wait until tragedy strikes before becoming active in searching out answers and solutions to your child's condition. Learn to anticipate possible snags your child might face at school, church, in the neighborhood, and at other social gatherings. Then make plans to avoid or creatively deal with these troubling situations. Inform those in leadership of your child's problem. As much as you are able, educate your child's teachers, coaches, and club leaders. Offer your assistance whenever possible.

Caroline made several visits to the school where her daughter, Kendra, would attend in the fall. Caroline checked Kendra's classroom, searched out the cafeteria, and walked the halls where Kendra would be riding in her wheelchair. She spent time getting to know Kendra's teacher and the administrative staff. Once Caroline felt comfortable, her next step was to introduce Kendra to these new surroundings.

- **Locate the best medical care available.** Inquire at local hospitals, visit several doctors, medical centers, support groups, schools, libraries, Internet sites, etc. Put the word out among friends and acquaintances that you're looking for information on the most current research being done and the latest drugs and therapy being used. Read up on the subject thoroughly. Keep a record of important advances and set-backs. Arm yourself with enough knowledge to make the best possible choice medically available for your child. Then be tenacious in going after it.

- **Select hobbies and sports where your child can excel.** Study your child's interests and skills. Discuss different areas of involvement available to your child, given your family's financial and scheduling resources. Look into several options and decide upon one to start. Make your child aware of the commitment required. Unobtrusively guide your child toward an area where he can succeed if he applies himself.

Felicia's daughter Alyssa had been injured in a car accident which had paralyzed her from the waist down. Aware of Alyssa's artistic bent and of her desire to help others, Felicia enrolled her daughter in a ceramics class. Alyssa spent two afternoons a week working on delicate ornaments and figurines which she excitedly gave to the nursing home residents where her grandfather was living.

- **Explore outside interests and take care of yourself.** Realistically deal with your own limitations. Honestly assess your physical and emotional limits. Show kindness to yourself. Take a few hours each week to pursue your own avocations. Understand that to be the best parent you can, you must remove yourself from the constant pressure of meeting the needs of your family. Especially, take care to get enough sleep, eat healthily, and exercise regularly.

At the crack of dawn, Dory is downstairs and exercising for forty-five minutes each morning. By the time she has exercised, showered, and dressed, her children are just waking up. Dory feels energized and satisfied that she's already accomplished something worthwhile so early in the day.

- **Be positive.** Remind yourself by way of 3 x 5 cards, daily calendars, and inspirational sayings that your child is special. Dwell on the simple joys of everyday living. Keep a joy journal and write in it each day. Live each day fully. Refuse to fall into the habit of worry. Search for the good in each circumstance.

Denise doesn't get out of bed in the morning until she's taken a few minutes to read and meditate on her daily proverb from the Bible. She reads it through once, and then a second time. Denise finds at least one verse to claim for herself each and every day. Armed with the strength of God's Word, Denise feels more prepared to face any challenges that may come her way.

Parenting is a journey. Sometimes the road is smooth, but often the road is peppered with bumps, and detours loom in front of your eyes. Before you plunge ahead in an attempt to correct a painful circumstance, take some time to consider, to reevaluate, and to pray. Develop realistic expectations of your family. Then trust God to meet your needs and theirs.

9

Positive Outlook:

Instilling a Great Attitude

in Your Child

T he recess bell had just rung. All eighteen pairs of feet dashed
out the side door for their thirty minutes of playground time.
Every pair except the pair belonging to seven-year-old Jared
who remained sitting at his desk. He looked a sight. His lower lip was
quivering, his eyes blinking in an attempt to hold back the tears. Jared's
teacher, Mrs. Winterfeld, sat at her own desk at the front of the empty
classroom, eyeing her pupil.

She wasn't sure what the problem was this time, but she knew one
thing. Somehow, little Jared had to be helped. All the school counselor
had told her was that Jared would be gone for a few days. That had been
over two months ago. Mrs. Winterfeld knew Jared's parents were getting
a divorce, so his few days away were probably right in the middle of that
nightmare. Poor boy, she thought with compassion.

She sighed, as she thought she knew something that might cheer
him up. Reaching into her storage container inside the deep confines of

her desk, Mrs. Winterfeld opened a box and pulled out a bright yellow smiley face bookmark. She rummaged through the box a bit more until she found a matching smiley face plastic wallet card. She smiled to herself as she reread the words printed on both the card and the bookmark: "Smile! God made you special!"

"Jared, can you come up here please?" Mrs. Winterfeld requested kindly.

Stifling his sniffles, Jared slowly walked up to his teacher's desk. His eyes pooled with tears, his hands fidgeted, and in a barely audible voice he said, "Yes?"

"Here." His teacher handed him the bookmark. "I want you to have this."

Taking the bookmark in his hand, Jared wiped his eyes. He studied it. He looked at Mrs. Winterfeld. He looked back at the bookmark. "Why am I getting this?" he asked.

"Look carefully, Jared. Let me read the words to you. They say, 'Smile!' Now, Jared," she coached, "I want you to smile. Come on, smile for me."

Jared, puzzled but wanting to comply, did smile. True, his smile was a bit crooked and not too exuberant. Still, it was a beginning.

"Good! Now, let me read the rest to you. 'God made you special!'" Mrs. Winterfeld explained. "This is exactly why I'm giving you this bookmark. To remind you how very special you are to me and to God." Jared nodded his head as he studied the bookmark again. "But, Jared, look. Do you see the smiley face card I have in my hand? It's exactly like your bookmark. Can you see it has the same happy face and the same words written on it?"

Jared nodded again.

"Now, Jared, this is very important. I want you to place your bookmark in one of your school books. I'm going to keep my card. But each morning when you come into the classroom, I want you to look up on the chalkboard for my smiley face card," she said pointing the board. "Every time you see my card on the board, you'll know I am praying for you, and my heart is smiling inside because you're part of my class. Do you think you can remember that?" she asked.

"Uh-huh. I'll look up there first thing after I put my coat away," Jared said with new conviction.

"Good. You keep your bookmark and learn to read the words yourself, all right?" Mrs. Winterfeld said warmly. "You're learning to read so quickly. It won't be long before you'll be able to pick out a whole bunch of books at the school library."

With tears dried and cherished bookmark in hand, Jared started back to his seat when he spun around. "Mrs. Winterfeld, can I take this home with me? I know my mom would like to see it too. I think," he said in complete earnestness, "that she'd like to know she's special too."

"Of course you can. You do that," his teacher encouraged. "Oh, but Jared, it will mean more to your mom if you're wearing a big smile on your face when you show her the bookmark, okay?"

Jared responded with spirit, "Okay!"

Mrs. Winterfeld watched her young student, so tender in years and experience, carefully, almost reverently, place his bookmark inside his reader. He started for the side door, took a parting glance back toward her—and smiled.

Breaking into a smile herself, Mrs. Winterfeld looked down at the card she still held in her hand. She opened the drawer to her desk once more and removed a bright yellow tack. She pushed the tack into the upper edge of the card and securely pressed it into the chalkboard. There, she thought, it's in place and ready for Jared's return. Sitting back at her desk, Mrs. Winterfeld bowed her head in prayer, remembering her solemn covenant to lift up the needs of one little boy to the care and keeping of a loving God.

Emotions like sadness, anger, and disappointment do not surprise God. As adults, we are often concerned with our children's so-called "negative" emotions. We fear that if our son or daughter is evidencing less than positive attitudes, we must be remiss in our parenting. Where are all those happy attitudes? we wonder.

Yet, God created us with emotional capacities which naturally run the full gamut. In the same vein, our children's attitudes affect these ever-changing emotions. By gently nurturing the right attitudes in our sons and daughters, we can thereby influence emotions, change behavior, and set in place righteous patterns for living.

Little Jared was feeling troubled and overwhelmed by the confusing circumstances brought on by the divorce of his parents. Everything around him was shifting, and nothing seemed stable. So, in the only way he knew how, he expressed his doubts, fears, and frustrations through his tears and displays of sadness. Who wouldn't be sad during a time of adjustment such as a divorce? While Jared wasn't aware of the fact, his teacher wisely honed in on a simple way to help improve his attitude. She showed him how to focus on the positive rather than the negative by using a tangible reminder—a colorful bookmark with a happy face on it. It worked. Within a few minutes, Jared went from feeling distraught and downhearted to feeling hopeful and encouraged. Best of all, Jared moved from desperately needing encouragement to being able to impart this important gift of hope to another hurting soul, namely his mom.

No matter what their ages, your children, like Jared, will go through times of feeling discouraged, disappointed, and disillusioned. Expect fluctuations in attitude and actions. Be prepared for them by prepping your kids in advance. Work consistently on developing positive attitudes that embrace an unknown and uncertain future with faith. As you read through the suggestions which follow, feel free to alter and adapt the principles according to your family's individual needs and interests. Remember, developing a positive outlook can be a good experience—it's all in your attitude.

Steps Toward a Positive Attitude

• **Make the Bible your standard.** Sit down with your children in the evening. Read aloud one of the following portions of Scripture each evening this week:

- ° The Beatitudes in Matthew 5:2–11
- ° The Lord's Prayer in Matthew 6:9–13
- ° The Fruit of the Spirit in Galatians 5:22–23
- ° The Love Chapter in 1 Corinthians 13:1–13.

Discuss and dissect the principles and promises line by line. Consider why each is an important character quality or attitude to internalize and exhibit. Memorize one verse per week. When all of you have memorized an entire section, have a we-did-it celebration.

Each of the Halman children raised their glasses of fruit punch and toasted their accomplishment. Within six months, Jenna's three kids had memorized two entire chapters of the Bible. As promised, Jenna brought home punch and a fancy cake to help celebrate their achievement.

• **Give thanks together.** Instruct each child to think of something he or she is thankful for. The sky's the limit! Kids may be thankful for a new friend, for a good test grade, or for not blowing their top at a sibling. Take turns offering up to God one-sentence prayers of thanksgiving for each item presented. Celebrate with popcorn or ice cream.

• **Play Bible charades.** Write down simple Bible stories on slips of paper and place them into a bowl. For example, Jacob wrestling with God, or David slinging the stone at Goliath. Have children select one slip and act out the story. Remind children that the emphasis of the acting should be to get across the Bible character's attitude. Discuss the outcome of each character's attitude and how it helped or hindered the plan of God.

• **Spend time reminiscing.** Ask your children to recall both happy and sad events from their past. Help them to relive a moment by role playing the scenario in brief. As you're retelling the story, challenge your children to think about how they, and others, felt during the episode. What positive or negative attitudes did they or others exhibit? Were these attitudes and actions pleasing to God? Why or why not?

Spreading the butcher block paper on the kitchen table and passing out markers, Carla asked her kids to recall one fun family event. For the next hour, each of them drew and colored differing aspects of this happy experience. Their combined efforts resulted in a kaleidoscope of colors and perspectives.

• **Read inspirational books.** Choose titles depicting godly heroes or heroines, as in books by Patricia St. John, C. S. Lewis, or other Christian children's authors. Talk about the characters' attitudes and how those attitudes affected their lives. From 8:00 to 8:30 A.M., Morgan reads a pair of chapters from a favorite book series to her children. Frequently her kids beg for more, but Morgan remains firm. Two chapters a day is the limit.

• **Design a "Happy Face" chart.** When a child has accumulated ten stickers within one month, award a small prize. Young children as well as teens will get into this game if you adjust the prize to their age-related interests. June created a blank calendar for each child and purchased multi-colored happy face stickers. When she observed a positive attitude, she placed a sticker on that date.

• **Study Bible heroes who display godly attitudes.** Review the tremendous obstacles that David, Jacob, Noah, and Esther overcame. Remind children how all of these heroes turned to God to give them the positive attitudes and the strength to do what was right. For example, Valerie hands each of her daughters a piece of paper with the first sentence of a story written on it. They are given five minutes to write the remainder of the story which might feature any number of biblical characters. Each girl then reads her story aloud to the rest of the family. Next, they enjoy ice cream sundaes as they discuss their stories.

• **Watch Christian videos which demonstrate character development.** Bonita did this when she instituted a family night. Every Tuesday she and her children would watch a family movie and then discuss it over an inexpensive treat.

Try movies that both entertain and instruct, such as those distributed by Feature Family Films. Play the Sticky Situations game produced by Focus on the Family which helps youngsters make godly choices.

10
Fostering Independence:
Balancing Protectiveness with Faith

*T*welve-year-old Katherine felt sure she was going to be sick. Purposefully, she refused any breakfast that morning. She nearly got out of the house with an empty stomach. But her mom stopped her and forced her to eat a piece of toast. Katherine had tried to explain to her mom that it was not a good idea for her to eat that morning. Not one single bite. Especially not today.

Katherine had been anxiously eyeing her calendar and crossing off the days in sheer terror for the last five weeks. At 10:30 A.M., Katherine was to play a flute solo for her school assembly. She was one of six students selected for the privilege. "Privilege, ha!" muttered Katherine, "I did everything but get down on my knees and beg to be excused from this."

Leaving the house, Katherine tried to console herself as she walked to school. What was the worst that could happen? Well, she might just miss a couple of notes. Or, she might really mess up and everyone would start booing her. Even that last chilling thought didn't disturb Katherine nearly as much as her secret fear. She tried, in vain, to steer her thoughts in another direction. Before she knew it, Katherine was reliving the first time her stomach caused her total embarrassment.

This momentous event had occurred several years earlier when her mom dropped her off at their new babysitter's home. Katherine could still remember the most absurd details of that afternoon. It was hot in the car as they drove to Mrs. Reed's. The bottoms of her legs stuck to the vinyl seats. Whenever she moved them, it felt as though she was pulling two suction cups loose. Katherine also remembered the smell of Mrs. Reed's house. A strong musty odor mixed with a sickening sweet floral air deodorizer permeated the entire home. Mrs. Reed, Katherine knew, went to their church, and although Katherine couldn't exactly pinpoint who Mrs. Reed reminded her of, it wasn't someone pleasant. Katherine got the distinct impression that Mrs. Reed was helping her mom only because she thought all men were bad people. She even commented to Katherine and her brothers that they would all be much better off after their daddy moved away. Then it happened. Her breakfast and mid-morning snack came up and was strewn all over Mrs. Reed's living room floor. The next few minutes, Katherine, thankfully, couldn't remember too clearly. She did recall that they were never again dropped off at Mrs. Reed's house.

"Oh, why me?" she moaned. "Other kids just bite their fingernails or tap their feet when they're nervous. Me, I have to throw up. It isn't fair."

As Katherine neared her school she spotted her good friend Megan. Waving Katherine over, Megan said, "Today's the big day, huh? Are you excited? I think I'm going to just die. I mean, if my dad wasn't threatening to take away my allowance if I didn't play today, I wouldn't even think of going through with this . . ." Chattering incessantly, Megan's words made Katherine feel that much more queasy. "Is your mom coming to watch you today?" Megan asked.

"No, she can't get off from work," Katherine replied with resignation.

"Oh, that's too bad. But I'm sure they'll be taping the whole program. You can ask for a tape from Mr. Kendall," Megan suggested eagerly.

"Yeah, I guess," Katherine replied. "Well, see you later." Katherine listlessly walked to her first class. Throughout the entire hour, she forced herself to remain focused on the math lesson at hand. At 9:30 A.M., the bell rang. Katherine made up her mind then and there. She'd never agree to play a solo again. It wasn't worth this agony of anticipation.

Dismissed from her regular English class to practice before the assembly, Katherine and Megan met each other coming into the band room. Megan squeezed Katherine's arm in shared excitement. Each of the soloists were to take turns warming up and playing their selected piece before the rest of the band members. When Katherine's name was called, she felt a sudden rush of panic. She also felt the contents of her stomach lurching to and fro. Standing up, she bolted from the room.

Thankfully, the girls bathroom was adjacent to the band room. Katherine didn't get sick. But she stood there waiting for the inevitable to either proceed or pass. Feeling foolish, Katherine didn't know how to gracefully reenter the band room. Wiping the clammy moisture off her hands, Katherine took a deep breath and prepared herself for the knowing looks that were sure to come. "Katherine, wait!" Turning around, she saw her mom half-running down the hall. "Am I late? Did I miss you playing?" she asked.

"Oh, Mom. I just can't do it," Katherine cried.

Katherine's Mom put her arms around her and tried to offer some small measure of comfort. "Katherine, I'm so proud you. I know you can do it," she reassured. "I'll be sitting out there praying for you, too. You know I will. Can we take a minute to pray somewhere quiet?"

Looking around, Katherine pointed. "No one's in the bathroom now."

Leading her trembling daughter into the bathroom, Mom prayed for Katherine. She asked God to provide courage, strength, and calmness. When she finished, Katherine's mom said, "You know, I wasn't supposed to be here today. But Jeff called and said he wouldn't be coming in until after lunch, so I could take off for an hour or so. I know God answered my prayers in allowing circumstances to work out for me to be here. Won't you try to trust God to give you what you need to play your flute today?"

Tilting her head to one side, Katherine sheepishly looked into her mom's eyes. "Mom, how do you always know how to get me to do what you want me to?" she asked with a slight grimace.

"Experience," Mom replied. "Don't forget, I used to be the girl who wet her pants every time something got me excited."

"Oh, Mom, don't remind me," Katherine groaned.

"And you thought your nervous habit was embarrassing!"

We've all felt it—that surging sensation of nervousness deep in the pit of our stomachs brought on by the mere thought of an unfamiliar or unexpected event. Adults and children alike experience this uncomfortable moment in time when the "fight or flight" mechanism takes over. But a little preparation and a little prayer can make a mighty difference in our willingness to expand and explore our world.

And so it is with our children. As moms, we must learn to look ahead and anticipate any possible snags and snares, thus wisely paving the road ahead for our children. In this way, their journey, while peppered with occasional bumps, won't leave them permanently detoured and dangerously disabled.

Katherine's mom knew how nervous her daughter felt. She also recognized that trying something new, experimenting with developing skills, and meeting unexpected challenges are all part of growing up. While Katherine's mom would have given the world to save Katherine from suffering, she dared not. She knew, as only a mother can, that Katherine needed to face these small challenges that come as part of childhood. By helping our children face their fears and insecurities as youngsters, they slowly, at times painstakingly, develop the strength and resilience to overcome larger obstacles as budding young adults.

Today or tomorrow, your child will be brought face to face with the unknown and the uncertain. How will you respond? Will you choose to wisely prepare your child for life by gently encouraging age appropriate independence? Every mom should aim for that fine line of distinction which falls somewhere between overprotectiveness and a letting go tempered by faith. Whatever stage of parenting you find yourself in, look ahead, anticipate possible problems, and build a sense of confident expectation into your children's hearts and minds. Let them know you'll always be there for them. Children will reach farther and with more gusto, if they're confident that you're standing behind them and their efforts. Together you and your children can face the future with confidence and assurance.

How to Develop an Independent Child

- **Prepare your children for any schedule changes.** Review the calendar and discuss any deviations in the routine. Explain how the schedule will be altered and what events will occur. Patiently answer any questions your child may pose. Eliminate as many unknowns as possible.
- **Select caregivers who care.** Search out adults who express love in a gentle, tender manner. Look for those who get down to the child's level and who understand the emotional needs of youngsters—their insecurities, and their interests. Give your children the opportunity to choose their caregivers, if possible.

Rhonda was faced with finding a new babysitter when her work hours changed. Rhonda's long-time babysitter wasn't available during the new hours. After a careful search, Rhonda narrowed her choices to two women. Rhonda invited each one over for dinner on separate evenings to observe their interaction with her children and to get her kids' thoughts on who they felt most comfortable with.

- **Check out the new surroundings.** Make several brief visits to the place where your child will be going. A quick look at a classroom, ball diamond, or daycare facility can dispel many of the scary unknowns a child secretly fears. Kids' imaginations are always working overtime. Allowing them to see their new surroundings with their own eyes will bring exaggerated fears back into proper perspective.

When Natalie moved to a different city, her sons were eager to get involved in community sports, but seemed a bit hesitant about joining new teams. Natalie drove her sons to the fields where they spent time running around, exploring, and hitting some balls. Much of their trepidation was reduced.

• **Enlist the help of a peer or sibling.** Whenever feasible, instruct older siblings or peers to take the younger children under their wings and show them around for a few days. Explain to your older "guides" what objectives you have in mind for your children. For example, Georgina hired the twelve-year-old neighbor, Mark, to show her son, Kevin, around his new school. Mark introduced Kevin to other classmates, ate with him at lunch, showed him where to find his locker, and generally helped break the ice for Kevin.

• **Give your children a "carry in my pocket" token gift.** This token might be a piece of jewelry, a photo of family members, or a sports memento. Leslie stashed a WWJD zipper pull into her daughter's lunch. She knew Sara was nervous about attending the sailing day camp. Leslie thought a little something from her might help remind Sara she wasn't alone.

• **Pray daily over fears and worries.** End each day with a time of family prayer, thanking God for all the good he has brought in your child's life. Then briefly ask for God's blessing for the following day. Make it a habit to discuss the day's happenings around your dinner table. Get other siblings involved and interested in each other's struggles and triumphs.

Nina used this idea. At her home, dinnertime meant good food and good conversation. Nina and her children learned early on to pray about everything they encountered. Good or bad, whatever topic was discussed around the table became the subject of serious prayer at bedtime.

• **Verbally uplift and encourage your children.** Regularly express the good choices your children make. Tell them how you appreciate their kind acts and unselfish behavior. Focus on the positive. Help your children build upon past successes. Slowly increase their responsibility and independence as maturity deepens and develops. Helen tried this and in less than a month, her daughter Callie had come out of her shell. Earlier Helen had recognized Callie's adeptness with small children and signed her up to volunteer in the church nursery. This accentuated Callie's budding confidence.

- **Memorize God's promises of protection and provision.** Select verses that speak of God's presence and protection. Memorize these verses together. Say them at night before bed and just before saying goodbye the next morning. Refer to 1 Peter 5:7 and Psalm 27:1. If your kids think memorizing is drudgery, try sitting cross-legged in a circle, each family member saying the next word of the Bible passage being memorized. Challenge one another to keep the words flowing fast. This technique can turn drudgery into laughing fits.

- **Instruct your children in social etiquette.** Teach your children how to introduce themselves to others and how to be introduced. Role play this skill at home and practice making conversation with adults and children with whom he is not familiar. For example, Heather dresses up right along with her daughters as they have a pretend tea party. Each one must be on her finest behavior, for all eyes and ears are waiting to disqualify another player. Whenever someone commits a social blunder, she's out.

- **Underscore the importance of being hospitable to outsiders.** Challenge your children to be sensitive to other children who are shy or friendless. Encourage them to reach out and invite newcomers into a game in progress. Remind your children how they felt when they first arrived and didn't know anyone. Instructions in empathy are priceless.

After working with her daughter, Jenny was pleased to see the results when daughter Jayne got out of her seat at church and invited a lonely-looking girl to sit with her. It warmed Jenny's heart to see shy Jayne take the initiative.

As we teach our children to rely upon God for their security, they will be able to go anywhere, anytime, and learn to adjust and thrive.

11
Best Friends:
Helping Children Form Positive Friendships

*E*leven-year-olds Joel and Tyler were identical twins. Few adults could tell them apart. Even their mom, Marisa, had to do a double take when she'd glance out to the driveway where the boys played their unceasing one-on-one basketball games. The twins were so similar in physical appearance that it often required concentrated behavioral observation to actually be sure who was who.

Of course, both Joel and Tyler thrived on playing the "guess who?" game with every adult they encountered. This guessing game was one of the two areas where Joel and Tyler agreed; the second was their mutual love for basketball. As similar as both were in appearance, Joel and Tyler were just as dissimilar in personality. Joel liked and thrived in school. Tyler's middle name could have been, "How can I get out of it?" Where Joel was responsible, Tyler was irresponsible. Joel was courteous and respectful. Tyler was continually pushing the limits with his smart remarks and sullen attitudes.

Marisa tried for years to figure out the best way to guide both her sons toward responsible living and respect for others. Joel, it seemed, didn't require any coaching. Sure, he occasionally blew it. But he'd come back with a repentant heart and accept the consequences. His conscience was keenly sensitive to even subtle attitudes and nuances that Marisa would send his way.

But that wasn't the case with Tyler. If Marisa didn't know differently, she would have insisted that Tyler didn't have a conscience. He could spout off any number of bold-faced lies and not flinch. Marisa frequently threw her hands up in despair over how to handle Tyler's deceit and willful wrongdoing.

When Marisa was called into the principal's office for the fifth time that semester, she knew something truly dreadful had occurred. She spotted the dean of students sitting beside her son. Internally, Marisa was quaking. What was it this time?

"Mrs. Stanton, Tyler's been suspended for three days," Principal Caldwell explained. "It seems he and another group of boys were fooling around with some chemicals in the chemistry lab while they were supposed to be eating lunch. They were trying to make some kind of explosive, or so they say."

"Oh, no," Marisa murmured.

"Yes, well. Nothing exploded, but the fire alarm went off. The entire school had to be taken outside while the fire crew came and put out the small fire," Mr. Caldwell continued, "and Tyler along with the other boys were seen running out of the lab."

Looking at her son, who to all outward signs appeared oblivious as to what the fuss was all about, just stared at his shoes. "Tyler, aren't you going to say anything?" Marisa demanded.

"Nothing to say," Tyler replied.

Dumbfounded, Marisa opened her mouth to say something, anything to help make sense of this fiasco. Pausing for a moment, she clamped her lips together and tried to muster up some semblance of dignity.

Sensing her distress, Mr. Caldwell asked the dean to take Tyler into the outer office. Marisa sat quietly, unsure, unsettled, and thoroughly unnerved.

"Mrs. Stanton, I don't want to upset you further but two of the boys Tyler was with today were found with knives. One of the boys was suspended all of last semester for a similar weapon offense." He added, "If Tyler were my son, I'd make certain he found different friends."

"Thank you, Mr. Caldwell, I appreciate your concern. I'll try to get through to Tyler," Marisa promised him and herself.

Leaving the office without giving in to the urge to shake her son silly took a great deal of inner strength. "Up and out," Marisa commanded. Momentarily submissive, Tyler quietly followed his mom's militant march to the car.

Once they were seated and belted in, Marisa turned on the engine. She was tempted to plead with her son to try harder, to be better, to live up to his potential. She was also sorely tempted to just sit in the parking lot and sob like a baby. Instead, habit came into play. Marisa backed out and headed toward home.

Marisa put away the thoughts of her son's rebellious behavior for a few minutes as she thought back. In the three years since her divorce, she had accomplished so much. The boys and she had moved to a smaller, older neighborhood. Even though their house was tiny, it had advantages. Located on the outskirts of town, it was surrounded by farm fields. Both boys spent countless hours running the fields with their dogs or hiking back to the small man-made lake beyond the fields to either explore, fish, or swim.

Way back when Marisa was still considering buying the house, she recalled her mom's comment about the boys being able to burn off their excess energy living here. Her dad agreed, saying it would keep them out of trouble. Apparently, Tyler was wired with more than his share of energy.

They had gotten the house. Then she'd been offered a part-time court reporting position. Marisa worked three days a week. She was grateful for the extra income, and she could still be home the other two days a week to get her household tasks completed. It gave her time with the boys, too, or so she thought.

Even though she got home an hour after they did, Marisa had to admit, she really didn't spend much time with them. They were off and running to neighborhood kids' houses or out in the fields. She wondered if there was some way to take back those lost hours, weeks, and months when Tyler was just starting to change and before he got into trouble? She should have been with Joel and Tyler instead of letting them run off on their own so much, Marisa thought.

Marisa wasn't sure if the damage could be undone, but she had to try. Right now, today, Tyler and she were going to see eye to eye on a few issues before he set one foot out of that door. She knew for sure his friends were going to change. That, too, was her fault. How many times did they beg her to drive them over to the Wallis' or the Kiefers' but she had pled exhaustion instead? It should come as no surprise that they'd made friends with these other boys. She hadn't left them any choice. She had also let their church attendance slide. She thought sleeping in on Sundays was no big deal, but what was she thinking? Obviously she hadn't been thinking much at all.

Marisa found out the hard way that children sometimes gravitate toward young people we adults consider undesirable. Youngsters don't have the same finely tuned ability to distinguish between acceptable imperfections and unacceptable ones. Thus, moms need to be keenly aware of their children's acquaintances before close friendships develop. We must also provide opportunities for positive budding friendships to deepen and grow under our ever-watchful eye of supervision.

In Marisa's situation, she realized too late that Tyler had gotten in with a group of boys whose influence was destructive. She'll need to spend a good deal of time and energy over the next months trying to overcome the negative influences of the past several years. As Marisa firmly sets the ground rules and reestablishes the importance of fellowship with other believers, she should be able to "take back" those lost periods of time which so negatively impacted Tyler. Joel, too, will reap the positive benefits of a more tightly knit family unit.

Who are your children spending time with right now? Do you feel comfortable with their choice of friends? Are you able to say you fully support the friendships your kids are developing today? If not, check out the methods outlined below which describe ways to enhance and strengthen your children's friendships.

Advice for Helping Your Child Pick the Best Friends

• **Lay a godly foundation.** Consistently stress the importance of selecting friends whose character God applauds. Share the biblical principle that while people look on the outside, God looks at the heart (1 Samuel 16:7).

• **Consider your children's personalities and be sensitive to their interests.** Trying to push your children toward children you admire but who don't have similar interests is doomed to fail. Keep your eyes and ears open for possible personality matches and invite a few friends over to visit.

• **Make like-minded friends available.** Make a habit of spending time in places where your child will regularly meet friends and develop friendships you can support. Attend your church's midweek programs. Or call around to local churches and take your children to participate in youth groups and ministries.

Christine made the effort to make sure her son got to youth group even though it often meant sitting afterwards in her car waiting for him. She learned to always bring an extra magazine or book. She was thankful he enjoyed coming each week to hang around with such a great group of young people and adults. It was worth her wait.

• **Terminate destructive friendships.** Be courageous enough to end any friendship that you believe is harmful to your child physically, emotionally, or spiritually. Explain the reasons why you will not allow him or her to spend time with this particular child. Talk it through, then pray for the well-being and salvation of such friends, if applicable.

• **Intercede continually.** Set the precedent of praying for and with your children. Ask God to protect them from ungodly influences. Pray that God will place a hedge of protection around your children at all times (Hos. 2:6–7).

After her children fall asleep, Mary Ellen walks from bedroom to bedroom and quietly stands outside her children's doors and prays for God to protect them. She rests easier each evening knowing she has deliberately committed her children to God.

• **Be a friendly neighbor.** Tell your kids they cannot play at a friend's home until you have met and become acquainted with the friend's parent(s). You may need to take the initiative to call and introduce yourself.

Lucy did this by having a party. She sent invitations to all her neighbors whose children were in the same age group as her own. She had a simple outdoor gathering with games and refreshments. By afternoon's end, Lucy felt she knew the other moms and their children well enough to make wise decisions regarding which families she'd feel comfortable having her children spend time with in the future.

• **Have a hospitable home.** Make your home a place that your children are proud of; a place that they can (and will want to) bring their friends. Encourage hospitality by setting the example yourself. Go out of your way to invite friends, coworkers and neighbors into your house. You don't need to plan a meal to be hospitable—coffee and cookies will normally suffice. Encourage your children to have friends in for lunch, to stay over all night and even go on outings with you. One little trick that kids will appreciate is buying extra snack food and hiding it from them in a secret, secure place. Then bring it out when friends are over. Kids love to know that mom's always prepared for company. Work hard to let your children's friends know that you love them and want them in your home.

• **Alert your children to potential snares.** A good general rule to follow: no television, videos, radio, preteen or teen magazines, to be watched, listened to, or read without prior permission from the parents of both families. Carefully explain the ground rules prior to allowing your child to spend time away from home. Remind your child frequently of the house rules.

• **Spare their feelings.** Unless you're willing to allow your child to spend the night at a friend's home, don't set the precedent by inviting that same child into your home overnight. Such a situation will only breed unwanted confusion and ill feelings. Danielle knew she couldn't encourage a close friendship with her daughter's schoolmate Trish. So, instead of starting something she couldn't follow through on, Danielle decided to stick to her decision and keep her daughter home. Despite her daughter's protests, Danielle knew it was the right thing to do.

Friendships brighten our world, add joy to our journey, and strengthen us when we're hurting. The wrong friendships can bring in untold heartache and pain. Moms need to teach their children to be a good friend as well as how to choose a good friend. Let your guidelines come from the Word of God. His principles will keep you and your family headed on the right path.

12

Sex Education:

A Tough Job, but Someone Has to Do It

*J*anice quickened her pace as she turned the corner toward home. Sweat trickled down her brow and back. Her breathing grew deeper. With a purposefulness bordering on the comic, Janice's countenance betrayed her. Normally after a four-mile run, she was tired, but a good kind of tired, one born of physical expenditure which drained the body of tension and the mind of cares. Today, Janice's muscles and nerves were every bit as taut as they were an hour ago before she had stretched. Pacing around the driveway while her heart slowed down to its normal pace, Janice continued to ponder the newest parenting challenge: explaining sexuality to her preteen daughter, Shelby.

Janice knew the day was fast approaching. She had tried to put it off. But this weekend she determined to sit down and talk with her daughter at length. Much to Janice's dismay, Shelby had been coming home from school with some naive misconceptions she'd overheard from her older classmates—the ones already wearing bras, assumed

Janice rather bitterly. Tomorrow or Sunday, she'd have to have that long-awaited talk. Then, it would be over. No more surprising assumptions or strange questions. They'd both feel better once they'd had a chance to hash all this out.

Gearing herself up for the big talk, Janice looked up at the kitchen window to see her daughter eating a Popsicle and smiling out at her. Suddenly all her resolve turned to mush. Feeling a bit weak, Janice smiled and waved back. Shelby was so young. Janice knew why she was resisting this discussion about sex. It was because she felt pushed into discussing it before she thought Shelby was ready. Who would have thought that so many nine- and ten-year-olds already knew the anatomical facts regarding procreation? She certainly never would have guessed it. Now, she was paying for her ignorance and so was Shelby.

Janice could still remember the day this whole area of sex and reproduction first took prominence in Shelby's mind. It was a crisp, sun-soaked afternoon when Shelby bounded through the door recounting her friend Taylor's stories. Stories, indeed. The yarns Shelby told her were filled with misconceptions. Where on earth had Taylor gotten these ideas? Why had she felt compelled to shatter her daughter's innocent naiveté with her callous remarks? Not only did Janice spend the rest of the evening dispelling those faulty theories, but for weeks afterward, poor Shelby was preoccupied by what her mom had told her. Was Janice ever thankful when Taylor's family moved to another state!

She knew Shelby's interest had been peaked when Janice tried to bring the subject up again during Christmas break. Of course, some kids were talking during lunch. Already in tune to the subject of sex because of Taylor's thrilling ideas, Shelby soaked it all in.

Since then Janice had read a couple of good books for kids Shelby's age. They explained sexuality according to God's plan and the authors had done an excellent job presenting this touchy subject with tact and class. Even she, probably the most conservative mom in the county, felt comfortable reading the text and viewing the sketches of the male and female anatomy.

She'd also written down scripture verses she wanted to share with Shelby and some questions she thought were important to consider. Shelby wasn't quite ten. Still, Janice wanted to be sure she'd done a thorough job sharing and explaining God's plan for the biblical enjoyment of sex and procreation. She'd already heard too many faulty bits and pieces. Janice needed to try to provide the whole picture for her daughter this time.

The next day Janice took Shelby to the mall. After some window shipping, they picked up sub-sandwiches and walked to a nearby park. Janice felt good about the location for their conversation. They were alone enough to talk without interruption, but there were still other things happening around them so the talk wouldn't feel too intense. As they watched the ducks and munched on the big subs, Janice removed a book on Christian sexuality from her purse and told her daughter that she wanted to discuss some of the issues in the book. She explained to Shelby that she desired to set a solid foundation regarding sex and the sexual side of growing up. They talked about some of Shelby's earlier faulty ideas. Janice shared some of her own experiences as a teenager— about becoming a woman and the temptations she had personally faced. Mother and daughter agreed to spend a few evenings discussing some of the topics in the book. As they headed toward the car, Janice put her arm around Shelby's shoulders and drew her close. "Darling, these are exciting days watching you grow up," Janice confided. "But to you, they might sometimes feel like frightening days. I want you to feel free to be open and candid with me as you mature into a young woman." Shelby seemed to understand.

Janice stopped by the florist's on the way home. She let Shelby pick out a stuffed animal placed around a bouquet of fresh flowers, a special remembrance of Shelby's introduction to adult understanding of her body. As an extra treat, Janice allowed Shelby to select some of those glittery balloons to go with the flowers too. It was a mom's way of saying, "Shelby, you are special to me . . . and you're special to God."

As Janice found out, sharing the facts of procreation and the principles God has outlined in his Word does not have to be a dreaded affair. Rather, planned outings such as the one Janice took Shelby on, can bring a mother and her children closer than ever. Even spur-of-the-moment discussions draw us nearer to our children if we're open, honest, and willing to seize each opportunity.

Consider trying some of the suggestions listed below as you plan to share that wondrous aspect of our humanity—sexuality. Though you may find yourself agonizing in advance, as Janice did, over such conversations with your children, remember they are essential. One way or another, your sons and daughters will piece together information about sex. On their own, they might even get the correct information. The question is, will they use the information appropriately? As you carefully plan, pray, and open the lines of communication, God most certainly will bring purposeful blessings.

Suggestions for Teaching a Healthy Attitude about Sex

• **Make thoughtful preparations.** Prayerfully determine what you want to accomplish in your discussions with your child. Consider your child's age, temperament, and maturity. Do your research and select several good books, videos, or audio tapes to listen to privately. Then share these with your son or daughter. Decide how to broach your subject. Role play your conversation with a friend if you feel uncomfortable winging it. Write down any key Bible passages you want to read with your youngster. Make out a tentative schedule to follow. Your child will feel more at ease if you move the time along with flexible direction.

• **Choose tasteful, appropriate surroundings.** Atmosphere is important. Select a semi-private place such as a restaurant with booths, a park or beach, museum or zoo, or even a table at an isolated part of a shopping mall food court. The key here isn't total seclusion. Your child will probably welcome some noise and distraction as long as they don't interfere with your conversation. Make it a point to choose a place that you'll want to remember. A location with perhaps some special significance to your child or family will add to the memory. Add a fun activity. Shooting some baskets or hitting a bucket of balls while conversing helps relieve stressful moments for boys. Girls might enjoy window shopping or going out to lunch as part of their special time out with mom.

For example, every spring Dorinda treated her sons to the opening game of their city's minor league baseball. This year was a bit different. After their annual game, Dorinda took her sons to a nearby park to hike. Once she had them away from the busyness of the day, Dorinda spread her blanket on the ground and took out her Bible. She had prepared a checklist of what she wanted to discuss with her sons. Once they were back in the car, Dorinda handed each of the boys a wrapped package which contained a Christian book on sexuality for teens along with a contemporary Christian rock music CD. After they read the book, they could play their CD.

• **Organize your resources ahead of time.** Organizational skills were Jennifer's weakest attribute, so she met with her good friend Elaine. Together they hashed out a workable plan for Jennifer to follow as she prepared to talk with her daughter. Elaine shared how she had brought up the sensitive subject of sex with her (now adult) children. Jennifer felt she gleaned some tried and true ideas from Elaine's experience.

• **Create a memorable moment.** Kerri's daughter, Lizzie, found the whole concept of sexual intercourse both embarrassing and disgusting. Kerri was having a difficult time overcoming her daughter's "let's not talk about it" attitude. One afternoon, Kerri pulled out old baby photos of Lizzie and her brother. As Kerri relived the excitement of giving birth, Lizzie realized what a miracle new life is. That day Lizzie admitted that just maybe God had created sex for a useful purpose.

• **Keep a positive, godly attitude.** Your attitude about sexuality will in great part determine your child's perception. Remember that God has ordained sexual union and has given sexuality as a gift. He has blessed our sexuality. It is our fallen world that has tainted this blessing. Provide

God's plan for purity prior to marriage and outline his guidelines for sexual union within the context of marriage. Explain the responsibilities that growing up and sexuality encompasses. In an upbeat manner, describe the cause and effect of living in a way pleasing to God versus going our own way. Share honestly the repercussions of disobedience—disease, pregnancy, and broken trust.

• **Follow up with discussion and questions.** Once your time together has concluded, don't neglect to set future dates for further discussion. Commit to reading a book together that deals with the ethics of responsible Christian living and explores Christian womanhood or manhood. Ask questions to gently probe into your child's ideas and understanding. Continue to keep the communication lines open with spontaneous, single-question moments that can occur anytime, anywhere. Be available to your child and let him or her know that you are.

• **Bathe the process in prayer.** Prayerfully determine the timing, the content, and the method to employ when sharing sexuality with your son or daughter. For example, Gerry knew the importance of a prepared heart. She spent an extra thirty minutes in prayer before bed for a full week prior to opening the subject of procreation with her son.

Ask for the Lord's guidance in preparing both you and your child for this special time. Remember that God has instituted the sexual union of husband and wife and this part of our lives has his approval. Pray for the leading of the Holy Spirit before, during, and after you spend time with your son or daughter. It will be time well invested.

13

Midlife Changes:

Facing and Embracing Your Future

As we stood apart from the crowd huddled around the blazing campfire, my good friend's words took me by surprise. "Midlife . . . What did you say?" I asked with sharp interest. Straining to hear her answer, I leaned forward, trying to hear her over the happy campers' songs. First, because I did not feel like a happy camper. Second, because I was searching for some answers to my own questionable emotions of late.

My friend leaned toward me and in a fugitive's whisper, confided, "I feel like I'm going through a midlife crisis."

"You're kidding," I responded with a knowing smile. "Tell me about it."

As this dear friend began explaining her symptoms, I realized with great relief that I wasn't alone. I wasn't losing my faculties at the ripe old age of thirty-eight. Nor was I the demented mother I had painted myself out to be only hours earlier. I was normal. And I came to this conclusion by commiserating with another woman feeling the same emotional swings, intellectual struggles, and spiritual questions that I had been experiencing these past months.

After lengthy conversation, I felt relieved. Yet I wondered just how many other friends and acquaintances were dealing with similar issues. I mentally took note of the women whom I know and considered their stresses and current struggles. Piece after piece of an intricately woven puzzle started to take shape.

Kari, a single mother of three, went through a deep depression in her late thirties after adjusting to a series of moves from state to state. She fluctuated significantly from having thoughts of suicide to feeling moments of great contentment. From one day to the next, Kari never knew what to expect from herself. She would wake up one day feeling on top of the world, eager to continue her important work at a nearby hospital emergency room. The following day, she could barely muster the energy required to get out of bed and into the shower. If it wasn't for the fact that she needed a paycheck to survive, Kari would have allowed her listlessness to overtake her better sense, and she would have stayed in bed every day.

Realizing that something was dreadfully wrong, Kari sought out a respected colleague and confided in her. Over several months, Kari regained her energetic self again. At the advice of her doctor, she started a consistent regimen of exercise combined with a natural hormone replacement treatment. Her doctor warned Kari not to expect too much too soon. But Kari was feeling better physically and more emotionally balanced within three weeks' time. The stress she'd experienced from relocating over the past eight years, not to mention her adjustment to divorce and single parenting, had caught up with her. Kari was also entering that peri-menopausal stage when her hormones were taking on a life of their own. Once she understood what was happening on the inside of her, Kari provided her body with the tools required for optimal strength and good physical health. As she began to heal and repair physically, Kari was better able to cope emotionally and mentally with all the exterior pressures she had to face.

Sheryl, another single mom of two in her late thirties, experienced great restlessness and an urgent drive to make major changes in her life. She even contemplated dropping her children off at her ex-husband's home and leaving the state. Sheryl was uncharacteristically filled with surging cycles of resentment toward her ex-husband. She loathed the fact that he was successful in his beloved career while their divorce forced her to reenter the job market at an entry level position.

Sheryl dearly loved her children. Still, she fought against a part of herself that was jealous of her ex-husband's freedom and professional accomplishment. Although she recognized the fallacy of thinking she had wasted those years living as a wife and mother, Sheryl also realized she would have achieved more professionally and personally if she'd not been in the home all those early years. Sheryl's body, too, was changing and preparing itself for menopause. As she tried to maintain her rigorous schedule of working, home ownership responsibilities, and solo parenting, she was left with little time to care for her own physical needs. Like Kari, Sheryl should have started taking care of her body and researching the newest treatments for women entering this middle age phase of life, but she didn't.

Instead, Sheryl continues to battle her resentment, her ex-husband, and her body. She also continues to fight the slow decline of her energy level and physical stamina. Sheryl's body, in desperate need of proper care, is sending out warning signals, if only Sheryl would take heed. Over time, she may find herself unable to cope with life's pressures because she's not taking steps to protect and enhance her health today.

While each woman faced uniquely different circumstances, both felt and dealt with similar struggles and issues. Common to both Kari and Sheryl were these feelings: restlessness, lack of control over circumstances, frustration with the present, anxiety over the future, longing for more personal fulfillment, and desire for intimate relationships. They both caught themselves reliving past events, or reevaluating and questioning commitments made years earlier. Emotional swings, tearfulness, feeling cheated, and grief over unmet goals marked their days.

In each woman's mind, she felt her life had already peaked, and she was heading into a downward spiral. This fatalistic attitude only served to make the feelings more intense and volatile. Sadly, most women feel excessive guilt and also lack any genuine understanding as to why their emotions are taking such a roller coaster ride.

As I studied this difficult phenomenon, I appreciated an excerpt from the book *Women and Stress* by Jean Lush. From one of her studies Lush concluded:

> I could not imagine why energetic and very functional women were suddenly feeling lethargic and hopeless. Many were frightened about these changes and felt overwhelmed by ordinary duties they had successfully handled for years. . . . Now we understand more about the emotional phases of a woman's life. Typical symptoms associated with hormonal changes during the late thirties and early forties are . . . 1) a sudden drop in energy, 2) unusual irritability, 3) touchiness/overreacting, 4) mild depression, 5) loss of interest in highly valued activities. (Jean Lush, *Women and Stress*, Grand Rapids: Fleming H. Revell, 1992, 113,115.)

This sensitive time of hormonal change for women relates to both the physical and emotional dynamics of womanhood. Physically, hormonal changes begin as some women move toward early menopause. Moreover, monthly menstrual cycles continue to take their toll on women's mental psyche and physical stamina.

From a strictly emotional standpoint, this midlife questioning and reevaluating does indeed constitute a midlife crisis for many women. Women recognize that realistically half of their life may be over. They don't feel they have enough to show for their years on earth. As believers, we are to think in terms of eternity; thus we have the added burden of asking ourselves if we've made each day count toward the eternal. These are hard questions.

In fact, women are literally torn between their own feelings and desires and what others expect of them. As both Kari and Sheryl came to accept, they had to make decisions that forced them to choose between what they wanted and what they needed to do. During this time of tension and indecision, you may find yourself having to make some tough decisions, too. Looking toward the future with an eye on the past isn't necessarily a negative thing—providing that when we look back, we learn from our mistakes and use those life lessons to help us create a positive, fruitful future. The following suggestions include ways to lessen the burden you're now carrying alone.

Helps to Lessen Your Lonely Burden

• **Assess your situation from a practical standpoint.** List what you term as positive areas in your life. For example, good family relationships, valued friendships, an acceptable work situation. Then list anything you deem as negative or without benefit—concerns over children's behavior, unsuitable living conditions, poor health.

Once you have laid out on paper your pros and cons, you are ready to evaluate your life realistically. First, be thankful for the positives you were able to list. Second, study the negatives and find ways to change, improve, or accept each of them. Start with one area you want to change and work toward altering that single part of your life. As you notice improvement in that area, mentally plan the next avenue for change. When the time is right, implement your second phase for eliminating the negatives. Continue through your entire list. Be careful not to expect perfection. Life is always peppered with less than perfect relationships and circumstances. Still, we can always work to improve those troublesome sore points, and we feel better in the process.

When Debbie tried this, she listed five things that happened that week for which she was grateful. Next, she wrote down one area where she had really blown it. Under that, she wrote her game plan for the next time a similar situation arose. A year later when she read over her journal entries Debbie was pleasantly surprised to see how much she'd grown.

• **Examine your goals.** Again, use pencil and paper to list any and all goals you have already accomplished. Next, list any goals you still desire to meet in the coming months and years. Dare to dream as you design your long-term goal sheet. Do you want to complete a college degree? Have you been wanting to get involved in local politics? Are you interested in community service work? Is there a major redecorating job you have simmering in the back of your mind? How about traveling to some distant locale? Whatever your heart's desire, make a plan to reach that goal. It may be financially impossible to implement plans tomorrow or even next year. However, with a long-term goal in mind (and on paper), you can gain the encouragement and confidence necessary to keep plugging along even in the face of setbacks.

Mindy had a dream of attending a summer workshop for herbal gardeners. Her own gardening club highly recommended this week long time of concentrated study and hands-on projects. In order for Mindy to attend, she'd have to save enough to make up for the lost work time. Mindy calculated the expense of the class and the amount of money she'd need for that week for household expenses. By mid-May, Mindy had reached her goal.

• **Keep in close touch with trusted friends.** Never isolate yourself from the loving concern of others. Allow yourself to be loved and pampered by committed friends and family members. Be honest and open with your family. Explain your feelings, kindly. Let your family and friends know that you don't blame them for your emotional funk. As you take time to share with those close to you, you may find more sympathy than expected. Simply unloading on a good friend can do wonders for your emotional state in struggling through midlife woes.

Forty-year-old Gloria felt unable to cope with the demands of her life. Wisely, she reached out to her women's Bible study group for help. They came to Gloria's rescue. In rotation, each of Serena's friends took a different day of the week to check in with her. They'd call, drop by, or invite Gloria and her children over to their homes. Once Gloria got over the worst of her struggles, she acknowledged how instrumental her friends' consistent love, concern, and attention had been to her recovery.

• **Take care of your physical needs.** Each year, Hope faithfully makes her appointments for dental checkups, her eye exam, and her general physical and gynecological exams. She tries to set up the appointments on the same date so she's only disrupting her schedule for a single day. Hope realizes how important these checkups are. Her own mother died of colon cancer which the physician said could have been detected early through regular examinations.

Get enough sleep. Eat nutritious meals. Exercise. More than ever before, the time is right for making a concerted effort to take proper care of our bodies. When the emotional part of us is under strain, our bodies suffer. Adrenaline rushes can only last so long before the body starts to rebel and illness steps in to take its place.

• **Know when to get professional help.** In some instances, women need the kind of care only a professional physician can offer. Never take your mental well-being too lightly. If days go by without relief and a dark cloud hangs over you, set up an appointment with your physician or a capable Christian counselor. Be persistent. Get the help you need.

Debilitating migraines drove Jean into bed several days a week. Depression kept her there. Her children feared for Jean's mental health and called Jean's parents. Jean's mother and father drove across country to be with her and the children. They insisted on Jean seeing a medical doctor and got her into counseling at her church. Jean credits her folk's firm guidance as the first step in her healing process.

Finally, remember that all of life is changing. Each day contains possibility, each moment a new opportunity to usher in a better phase of life. As women, we need to recognize our potential and maximize each gift we possess.

What Failure Means

Failure doesn't mean you are a failure . . .
  . . . it does mean you haven't succeeded yet.
Failure doesn't mean you have accomplished nothing . . .
  . . . it does mean you have learned something.
Failure doesn't mean you have been a fool . . .
  . . . it does mean you had a lot of faith.
Failure doesn't mean you have been disgraced . . .
  . . . it does mean you were willing to try.
Failure doesn't mean you don't have it . . .
  . . . it does mean you have to do something in a different way.
Failure doesn't mean you are inferior . . .
  . . . it does mean you are not perfect.
Failure doesn't mean you've wasted your life . . .
  . . . it does mean you've a reason to start afresh.
Failure doesn't mean you should give up . . .
  . . . it does mean you should try harder.
Failure doesn't mean you'll never make it . . .
  . . . it does mean it will take a little longer.
Failure doesn't mean God has abandoned you . . .
  . . . it does mean God has a better idea!

                                        - Author Unknown

14

Blended Together:

Adjusting to Step-family Status

*F*orty-five-year old Judy was driving home on the freeway when she spotted a billboard hawking the services and skills of a well-known, downtown lawyers' firm. Judy did a double take as she read the words, "If you've been injured in an auto accident . . . contact our office day or night. Phone 419-555-0083." Below those oversized, fluorescent letters was a phrase written in bold, black lettering that caught Kara's attention: "No divorce suits; we handle serious injury cases only."

Judy fumed. That beat all. How much more seriously injured could one get than being involved in a divorce? Divorce cases, not serious enough? She shrugged off an impulse to drive over to that office and let those lawyers know how "seriously injured" one family can end up due to divorce. She could go over point by point how much she and the kids had lost.

In no particular rush to get home, Judy drove along the highway taking little notice of the passing drivers whizzing by her on either side. Kara's thoughts kept going back to that billboard advertisement. She was amazed that people didn't understand how truly horrible divorce was. She was glad it was in the past.

Even though she still harbored anger, life had actually settled into a comfortable routine. Twelve-year-old Evan and thirteen-year-old Grace were both doing fine in junior high school. Her job was going well, even though she wasn't too thrilled with her office's new location downtown. Then she'd met Allen, a father of one her children's classmates. She couldn't believe Allen was part of her life.

She never imagined she'd ever trust another man, let alone fall for one. But, he'd been a godsend since the first time they'd met at the kids' soccer match. Not only was Allen supportive and sensitive, he balanced his kindness with a solid sense of strength and integrity. He'd gladly help Judy with any problem she was troubled over. But, he knew where to draw the line. Judy wasn't seeing Allen through rose-colored glasses either. She had learned a lot from her first marriage. Allen wasn't perfect, but they were definitely compatible.

Judy chuckled. Between his kids and hers, they certainly filled a table when they dined out. Allen's kids were super, too. She wanted to grab them and give each of them a big hug whenever they walked through the door. But they might not appreciate that. Fifteen-year-old Chris and thirteen-year-old Dean were warming up to her and her kids. But nine-year-old Kelly still wasn't too sure about her. She sat next to her dad and held his hand coming in and going out. Hopefully in time, Kelly would come to accept that her mom and dad wouldn't be reconciling. Maybe then she'd draw a bit closer to her. Time would tell.

After Judy had experienced the ups and downs of single parenting for over five years, she realized she was finally ready to make a serious commitment to Allen. They had spent a good two years in each others'

company and were contemplating making the relationship a permanent one. Then Judy started having doubts as she and Allen discussed the practical aspects of joining their two households.

Questions and concerns loomed in Kara's mind. Just exactly how was she going to make a home for Allen's kids and her own? Would her children feel okay about this new arrangement? Would his? "What ifs" began to plague Judy until she decided that maybe she wasn't quite so ready after all.

When adults with children from a previous marriage begin pondering the possibility of joining their lives, the term "yours, mine, and ours" takes on a personal new dimension. No longer is it the funny tag line from an old comedy. It means sharing everything—your material goods, your time, your lives, and, most important to the children, sharing mom and dad.

As single moms and dads like Judy and Allen make plans for the future, they must determine which options encompass their children's best interests while considering their own needs and desires. Even Judy, the woman who swore to friends she'd never marry again, discovered some intense needs for companionship when Allen entered her life.

According to *The Journal of Marriage and Family*, 47 percent of all marriages involve at least one previously married spouse. Of men who divorce, five out of six will remarry; of women, three out of four will remarry.

Given that 50 percent of single moms and dads will remarry within the first three years after their divorce, single parent families have the burden of proof thrust upon them. Thus, the single parent who proactively rather than reactively faces each day and its challenges is the one who will find the future a place where fulfillment and satisfaction walk hand in hand.

Judy and Allen took a good deal of time talking over the nuts and bolts of combining their two families. They both agreed that of all the children, Kelly was the one who might pose some objections to their marriage. They decided to tell their respective kids alone, feeling them out and getting their input. Then they would gather the entire group together and really talk about joining both families sometime within the next year. Once Judy and Allen had these two family discussions, they would talk alone again and decide how to proceed.

Neither Judy nor Allen wanted to marry against the wishes of their children. Both knew they needed the full support of their kids to make their blended family a success. They also knew that it was unreasonable to expect a fairy tale ending once their families joined. With good preparation, a solid foundation of faith, and a willingness to commit selflessly, Judy and Allen's future looked hopeful and happy.

Have you considered the possibility of remarriage? Or do you feel, as Judy did prior to meeting Allen, that you cannot imagine ever making another commitment of marriage? Perhaps you're recently divorced and your wounds are still fresh. Maybe you're content and satisfied with your life as it now stands. In either case, read through the suggestions below —ideas for building healthy relationships, single or married, adult or child. Whatever relationships you may enter into during the coming months and years, preparation is essential for success. And success is measured by God's high standard, not by a shallow relationship rich in financial resources or emotional security alone. Better to remain a single woman with integrity and self-worth than a married woman who has compromised her values and standards in exchange for a temporary band of gold.

Things to Consider before Remarriage

• **Learn to trust again.** Remember when your child was learning to walk? He or she would take a step, fall back, get up, and take another step. Relationships, too, are a process. Model to your children acceptance and respect for others. Contemplate those in your life who've been faithful and build upon the proven trust they've shown to you. Use their faithfulness as the foundation to courageously reach out and make new commitments that have the potential to last a lifetime.

Eve didn't have the courage to enter into another relationship with a man. She had been deeply hurt by her ex-husband. Then she met Kent at their church's Single Again group. Kent had shown special interest in getting to know Eve better. Eve wasn't complaining. Still, she was wary. Eve's good friend Cameron gave her the best advice possible. Get to know Kent as a friend. Then relax and enjoy the relationship.

• **Take it slow.** Divorced only six months, Abigail ached to marry again. When an old family friend unexpectedly came back into her life, Abigail was delighted. She was also desperate. Fears and uncertainties tempted her to commit to this well-established, successful man who she didn't honestly love. At the advice of her friends and family, Abigail broke the relationship off. In her heart, she knew any future marriage had to have more foundation than financial security.

Many unhealthy attachments occur within the first months after a divorce. The great neediness in us comes out when we're hurting and we search after that "right" person to make the pain go away. By taking internal stock of yourself—strengths, weaknesses, values and priorities —you can better choose people you want to know more intimately as opposed to those who spell trouble for you and your kids.

• **Make proper introductions.** Robin and Christopher decided to explore and deepen their relationship. Now is the time, thought Robin, for my kids to get to know Chris better. So Robin and Chris set up a schedule for family time. Each Tuesday evening, they ate dinner together, and then Chris would attend the kids' soccer games. After the games, ice cream became a regular habit. This weekly routine gave Chris and Robin's children the opportunity to get to know one another in a variety of settings.

Most experts agree that formal introductions to the children needn't take place until both adults are ready to make a lasting commitment to each other. At that point, children should be brought into the relation-ship. Kids find it confusing and frustrating when a parent brings home a string of suitors. It's difficult for children to share a parent with mere casual acquaintances. However, if the children sense this new adult truly cares for their parent and is working toward a lifetime commitment, much of their internal stress is reduced.

• **Work out the snags.** Your daughter whines and cries whenever your date comes over to the house. You understand her insecurity. However, a deeper issue is involved here. Your child's actions and attitudes are falling short of the godly standard you've instilled in her. You must intercede and get to the heart of the matter. Privately, listen to your child's thoughts, reassure her of your love, and firmly remind her of your family's high regard for honoring God's Word in all relationships. Stand firm in your expectations that respect and courtesy toward all people are non-negotiables in your family.

Square dancing was the highlight of Anna Marie's week. Her partner, Derrick, was good company and a good friend. Still, Anna Marie's daughter Melinda regularly made a scene right as they were walking out the door. It took Anna Marie months before she had enough. Sitting her daughter down, Anna Marie brought her Bible out. Together they read the Love Chapter (1 Cor. 13). With no ready excuse on her lips, Melinda reluctantly agreed to work on displaying a more unselfish and kind attitude toward Derrick. Her mom held her to that promise.

• **Curb jealousy through acceptance and respect.** Yolanda takes great delight in every opportunity to introduce her children and her fiancé Daryl's children to others. It tickles her to watch Daryl's kids' faces when she proudly includes them as her own. Daryl's children have no doubts that Yolanda's love for them is both constant and enduring.

Resist the urge to unnecessarily point out which is your natural child compared with those of your prospective mate. Children need to be fully accepted and loved without the stepchild stigma. Take time to get to know each child individually and become knowledgeable in each one's interests and hobbies. Be the most vocal cheerleader you can be. Then evidence your support through attitudes and actions of respect and admiration.

• **Watch for subtle manipulations.** Kids can spot an easy mark better than most adults. Discern a child's attempts to become the wedge between you and your future spouse. Work at understanding the whole story and don't rely on one child's sole perception of a situation. Take time to communicate with your future spouse and children. Then develop the fine art of effective negotiating by refusing to answer insult for insult. Instead, return good for evil, thereby defusing potentially angry confrontations.

Ten-year-old Douglas was a master at instigating petty fights between his older and younger sisters. When his mom, Corey, decided to date a man from their church, Douglas felt he had new territory to conquer. One evening, Corey and Douglas were alone in the house. Corey sat her son down and let him know in no uncertain terms that she was well aware of his antics. Surprised by his mom's astuteness, Douglas gained new respect for Corey and his bent for causing trouble declined dramatically.

• **Build bridges to the absent parent of the children.** As you contemplate becoming a stepparent to your future spouse's children, don't neglect the noncustodial parents from either side. Make concerted efforts to see that each of the children has consistent opportunities to visit with the noncustodial parent. Speak in positive, affirming ways whenever kids share their excitement over a recent visit. Be excited for them and express enthusiasm unconditionally. For example, every other Sunday evening, Cheri knows she'll be listening to her daughter and son's weekend activities. Since Cheri's ex-husband, Will, takes the children every other weekend, Cheri has wisely consented to share in her children's excitement. She knows how much they love their dad, so Cheri nods her head, listens attentively, and does her best to share in her children's enthusiasm.

• **Take a lesson in flexibility.** Ups and downs are standard in parenting. Try to maintain an attitude of balance. Resist swinging on an emotional pendulum. Model a positive outlook for your children by helping them see life's disasters from the proper perspective. Say yes whenever

Top Blunders of Divorcing Parents

The American Academy of Matrimonial Lawyers ranked the top ten mistakes parents with children make during divorce. In order of frequency, they are:

1. Denigrating the other spouse.
2. Using the child as a messenger.
3. Interfering with visitation rights.
4. Sharing with the kids intimate details of the other spouse's infidelity or negative behavior.
5. Failing to pay child support.
6. Immediately introducing the child to the parent's new love interest.
7. Moving the child as far away as possible from the other parent.
8. Listening to the child's conversations with the other parent.
9. Having the child read all the legal pleadings or having them contact the attorney.
10. Having the child request money from the other spouse.

—*New Man Magazine*, March/April, 1999, p. 14

possible and offer little doses of hope and encouragement to your kids.

• **Give and take ... over the long haul.** At least once each month, gather everyone together to discuss the inner dynamics of family life. Set the ground rules in advance. Aim at civil words and gentle requests. Write down guidelines and try them. Be willing to adjust them as your family's needs grow and change. Assure your children that you and your future spouse are in it for the duration, regardless of circumstances.

For example, the first Thursday of every month, Juanita picks up pizza on her way home from work. After dinner is over, Juanita gets out paper and pen. Moving clockwise from person to person, she gives each family member the opportunity to share any problems. Juanita keeps a short written record from month to month, to monitor progress. Any topic is open for debate. The Peñas only have one rule. For every problem shared, the speaker must come up with a positive comment, too. This rule helps maintain a balance, so that no family member starts dreading the Thursday evening meetings as a time of partisan bickering.

• **Weigh the burdens against the blessings.** Diane debated long and hard about her upcoming marriage to Jonathan. No matter how hard she tried, Diane couldn't rid herself of needling doubts. Unable to move ahead until she was certain marriage was the best for her, Jonathan, and her children, Diane told her fiancé they needed to wait until she was able to sort things out for herself. She explained to Jonathan how unfair it would be to them to marry when she wasn't 100 percent certain it was God's best plan for their lives.

Dating and remarriage can be great for some. For others whose main focus in a romantic relationship is the alleviation of personal burden, remaining single is perhaps the best choice. Single parents have to weigh the gains against the potential problems in remarrying. Over time, true motives and desires reveal themselves. Better to patiently assess the relationship, than to take the path where fools rush in and deep regret follows.

15

Forgiveness:

Everyone's Divine Assignment

*L*auren, at the age of thirty-three, was wondering where her next paycheck would come from. Laid off from the hospital where she worked as an LPN, she couldn't believe this turn of events. Only a month earlier, it appeared as though her hospital was going to merge with the largest managed care facility in the area. But then she and a hundred others were told their jobs would last until the middle of the month. Period. Lauren was angry and bitter. After all, she went into nursing because of the job stability.

Each day after work, Lauren picked up her kids at their daycare center and mournfully wondered if they'd be able to go there much longer. If Greg hadn't walked out on her, she wouldn't have to face this.

Laying in bed that night, Lauren ruefully considered how the smallest event caused her stomach to churn these days. Even the most unrelated incident could make her relive the nightmare of her divorce.

If Greg had been open with Lauren and vice versa from the outset, their marriage might have made it. But neither one could face revealing scars they had from their childhoods. What Greg and Lauren didn't realize was that by not confronting their pain honestly and biblically, both brought these problems with them to their marriage relationship.

Throughout the six years of their marriage, Lauren found herself both withdrawing from Greg and punishing him for his seeming indifference toward her. The more he got involved with work, the more she drew away from him whenever he was at home. Feeling overwhelmed with the pressures of school and two toddlers, Lauren decided that for better or worse, she'd get Greg's attention.

During one of the classes she was attending at her local college, Lauren met another unhappy fellow student by the name of Jeremy. He understood exactly what she was going through. His wife was on the fast track at a nearby computer firm, a position which took her out of town weekly. Jeremy stayed home, worked on completing his degree, and cared for their nine-month-old baby girl. Jeremy not only understood Lauren's frustration, he fueled it. It didn't take long for the two of them to become inseparable.

Twice weekly, before, during, and after class, Lauren and Jeremy talked about their lives, their struggles, and their dreams. But most of all, each found sympathy in the other—someone who not only listened, but encouraged the ranting against his or her spouse. Neither Lauren nor Jeremy knew, but they were priming themselves for an all out war of confrontation that could destroy what little communication still existed with their mates.

After the spring semester ended, summer gave way to some distance between Lauren and Jeremy. In a sense, time away from a sympathetic ear helped Jeremy gain back his perspective. He and his wife were able to work toward a more amiable place in their relationship. But time away from her only source of comfort spurred Lauren on all the more. She frequently reminisced over the special moments she'd spent with Jeremy and compared him with Greg. By midsummer, Lauren was laying siege to Greg night and day. Tired from all the conflict, Greg left home. Lauren was left with an economy-size load of anger, bitterness, and self-loathing.

Greg picked up his kids on Friday and kept them until Saturday evening. He wanted to visit them during the week, too, but he couldn't bear to face Lauren and her continual complaints and accusations. Lauren, jealous of the special times her two children had with their dad on the weekends, filled the nearest available ear with her resentment. Sitting by herself on a Friday evening, she wondered why, after all she'd done, did she have to spend every Friday and Saturday alone?

As Lauren learned too late, forgiveness is essential to healthy, growing relationships. Even after the divorce papers are signed, forgiving those who've hurt us is still important. Forgiveness is so vital to a full life, that without it, nothing else will amount to much.

Anyone who has ever been wronged knows the surging adrenaline powered by righteous indignation. We've all been there. Somewhere along the line, each of us has been burned, and we felt the pain cut through us. So how can anyone of reasonable intellect take seriously the notion of forgiving the unforgivable? Loving the unlovable? Extending mercy instead of justice? Under the sun, there's only one reason for any of us to "forgive our debtors." Because Christ commanded it. Because he made it possible, we can make it so.

Like Lauren, you may feel that there is no possible way to forgive your ex-spouse. Maybe his actions have brought you nothing but unending pain and heartache. No one can argue that point. Still, unless we purposefully decide to follow Christ's example and his command to forgive, we are the ones who suffer. Detailed below are principles outlined in God's word. Though some are difficult to embrace, each one is solidly based on God's commands to his people. Read them carefully and prayerfully, be honest with yourself, and work toward total healing. When we take that final step and genuinely forgive the one who has hurt us most we will discover true freedom and blessed renewal.

Godly Principles of Forgiveness

- **Forgive the offender.** Colin was a wife beater. He was thrown in jail for assault more times than he could remember. In the courtroom, his ex-wife, Elise, looked into Colin's haunted eyes. She knew his past. She knew how he had been abused and neglected as a child. While this knowledge didn't excuse his behavior, Elise understood. God gave her the grace to forgive Colin. She'd never be the object of his aggression again, but it took her forgiving him for Elise to be truly set free.

- **Let God be the judge.** We have been created with an instinctive desire for justice because God is just. When we are wronged, we react with natural revenge and retaliation. But this is not God's response. We focus on our anger and try to equalize the wrong through withdrawal or payback. But another wrong does not fix the problem, "for man's anger does not bring about the righteous life that God desires" (James 1:20). Our model is found in Romans 2:4: "God's kindness leads you [and others] toward repentance."

  For the first two and a half years of her divorce, Elana plotted and planned ways to get even with her ex-husband, Kirk. While participating in a women's Bible study, she came face to face with her anger and with resentment that God said was sin. It was not negotiable. Elana begged God to enable her to forgive Kirk. As Elana trusted God to set things right, she was able to "walk away" from Kirk emotionally for the first time.

- **Forgive in order to be forgiven.** One baby step at a time, thought Shana, as she pleaded with God to release her from her hatred toward her ex-husband. In that moment, Shana took the first step toward lasting forgiveness. She admitted to God that her hatred was a sin against him. God helped Shana see her pain from a different perspective. He taught her to view her divorce through his eyes. In time, Shana's relationship with God meant more to her than anything. She wasn't about to jeopardize the peace she'd found through obedience for any amount of transitory self-pity.

We are commanded to forgive (Col. 3:13) and must recognize that our own forgiveness depends upon it (Matt. 6:9–13). God also designed our physical bodies to suffer under the root of bitterness that comes as a result of unforgiveness (Heb. 12:15) while hindering our prayers when we refuse to forgive an offense (Mark 11:25).

• **Release your hurts to God.** God expects us to come to him as a little child and complain when we're in trouble or hurting (Matt. 18:3). As we turn our struggles over to God, we must simply release them to Him who we trust to fix them (1 Pet. 2:23). Part of this relinquishment means not allowing feelings and thoughts of unforgiveness to brew. We must deal quickly and thoroughly with these emotions and responses (Eph. 4:26). Perhaps the most difficult step is to start praying for those who have despitefully used you. As you pray a blessing for your offender, God will heal your heart. Make a deliberate choice not to rehearse and dwell on the offense. Though we cannot forget the offense, we can choose not to focus on it.

Esther cried out to God to intercede in her heart. She felt as vulnerable as a newborn. Every time she remembered Joel, sudden and fierce resentment poured from her heart. So moment by moment, Esther recited favorite Bible verses. She clung to God's promises. Almost indiscernibly, Esther realized she hadn't thought about Joel in a whole hour, a day, and then a week. Hanging onto God's word remained Esther's key to successfully forgiving her ex-husband.

• **Make forgiving a lifestyle.** As we determine to make forgiving a lifestyle, we can learn to give up our demands for perfect behavior. In time, God will reveal his power and ability to bring good out of the most painful situations (Rom. 8:28). Every day, our heart and mind must view forgiveness as a necessary, ongoing act of our will as well as a spiritual decision independent of fickle feelings.

Ellie handled her emotions by pouring out her heart into her cassette player's microphone. She let it all out as she spoke her honest, true feelings into that machine. Then, she replayed it. Ellen prayed and asked God to make her clean again, to give her a fresh start, and to provide her with a heart full of love. As was her habit, Ellen then erased her message from the cassette and set the recorder aside until she needed it again.

- **Forgive for the children's sake.** Jessica bit her tongue and prayed. Her children had just come home from another visit with their dad. Little did they know how much it hurt for them to relay their dad's callous words about Jessica to her. Fully dependent on God's grace, Jessica responded calmly and tactfully. Her kids soon ran off to play, oblivious to their mom's inner struggle. Jessica thanked God for yet another small victory on the road to freedom.

Unfortunately for us parents, kids model what they see at home. If we're evidencing an angry, bitter attitude, they will learn to do the same. Thankfully, God gives us power to forgive and, thereby, model godliness to our kids (2 Tim. 1:7). As we release our bitterness, our children, who

---

The Facts on Forgiveness

- Forgiveness is not a feeling. It is a decision you make to obey God. God calls you to forgive no matter how you may feel.
- Forgiveness is a spiritual event between you and God.
- Forgiveness does not seek revenge, retribution, or restitution but gives the offense to the justice of God.
- Forgiveness often needs to be repeated, as new memories of old hurts may occur.
- Forgiveness is not the same as tolerance, denial, or minimizing a hurt. It is not saying that what happened was okay.
- Forgiveness is not the same as restoration of trust.
- Forgiveness does not use the past against the other person.
- Forgiveness does not depend upon the response of the other person.
- Forgiveness is without limits and needs to be done with thoroughness. Forgive all people for all things.

—Linda Brown. Used with permission.

know full well when we've been wronged, will witness our forgiving spirit, and it will spur them on to righteous acts in their own lives. We equip our youngsters to face a world of injustices in school, on the job, and in relationships by forgiving. Don't underestimate the powerful influence your own example of forgiveness can have on your ex-spouse via your kids and what they communicate to others about you.

Appendix

Funstarts: 201 Ideas for Enriching Family Fun

Fun Together Inside

- Have a chess or checkers marathon.
- Gather all the loose family photos and place them in photo albums. Decorate the albums with silly stickers and funny captions under individual photos.
- Empty all the sock drawers into one big pile in the living room. Have everyone dig in and pair up the estranged socks.
- Place charade ideas inside balloons, then inflate the balloons. Each person selects a balloon, pops it, and then acts out the charade for the rest of the family.
- Read bedtime stories by flashlight under the covers.
- Sponsor a family film fest. Rent or borrow several movies. Set up a kitchen concession stand complete with beverages, popcorn, and candy.

- Give each other facials using commercial mud masks. Do manicures and pedicures using glittery nail polish.
- Make an indoor tent city. Use tables, chairs, furniture, and sheets for covering.
- Sponsor a silly sports night. Each person makes up the silliest game possible and teaches the rest of the family to play.
- Do face painting on the entire family (including mom). Take pictures and send them to distant friends and family.
- String buttons on thread and make necklaces.
- Design a family motto T-shirt using puff paints, glitter, buttons, and old broken jewelry.
- Take turns reading the funny papers aloud at dinner time.
- Have a jigsaw puzzle contest. Distribute to teams or individuals puzzles having the same number of pieces, then race to see who completes their puzzle first.
- Buy a goldfish. Give it a sophisticated name. Keep it in a glass jar on your kitchen counter.
- Bring sleeping bags into the living room. Turn off the lights and take turns telling stories until bedtime.
- Have a topsy-turvy day. Do everything in backward order. Brush teeth before eating. Turn clothes inside out. Eat dinner for breakfast.
- Play Bingo. Purchase prizes at a local dollar store.
- Just for fun, set back all the clocks in your house two hours. Give the kids the extra time to play before bedtime.
- Rearrange bedroom furniture. Add posters or simply change decorations around to create a new look.
- Teach your children how to short-sheet a bed.
- Have a musical smorgasbord. For the entire day, put on a different type of music every hour.
- Bring out everyone's shoes. Polish and shine them together.
- Dress up your pet dog or cat in fancy hats, ties, coats, dresses, and gloves. Position them on a piece of furniture and take pictures. Have these photos blown up into posters.

- Find new and interesting shoelaces. Take out old, worn laces and replace them with new, colorful ones to dress up used tennis shoes.
- On a rainy, summer day, cut out assorted snowflakes from construction paper and use colorful yarn to hang them onto windows.
- Pick a color day. Wear one particular color all day. Read books with the same color binding. Play games with the chosen color on the box. Eat foods made up of this color too.
- Play "I found it first!" Instruct everyone to start searching for a long lost item when you say, "Go!" The first person to find the missing item gets a treat.
- Institute "I'm your chum day" when Mom pretends to be her child's friend all afternoon and does everything an age mate would do with the child.
- Borrow a joke book from your library. Take turns selecting and reading jokes to each other. Try hard not to laugh.
- Practice good phone manners by taping your children as they pretend to answer the phone. Replay the taped portions for further instruction.
- Play dress-up. I choose the clothes for you today and you choose my clothes for me. From head to toe, dress in the outfit selected by another family member. Courageously, go out to dinner wearing these outfits.
- Tuck the children into bed and turn out the lights. Ten minutes later, come back into the bedroom(s) with mugs of hot chocolate.
- Use large appliance boxes to create an indoor tree house. Decorate the boxes with magic markers or paint.
- Make sweet music together. Borrow a hymnal from your church and sing old time hymns a cappella or with piano accompaniment.
- Pass out old family pictures of great grandparents and great aunts and uncles. Give one photo to each person. Have them make up a story to go along with the photo. Then, tell the kids the real story behind the photo.
- Read the daily newspaper as a family. Discuss the current events.

- Have an ABC party. Choose one letter of the alphabet. Everything at the party must begin with that letter. For example: bubbles, balloons, bonfire, bon bons.
- Teach your kids Pig Latin and speak this way for an hour.
- Collect postcards from local stores and gas stations. Make up a scrapbook with these cards showing all the places your family has "traveled."
- It's your dime. Allow each child to make a ten minute long distance call to anyone he or she chooses.
- Write letters to music artists or favorite children's authors and request their autographs.
- Institute a no-sounds morning. Everyone must be quiet from 9:00 A.M. until noon. If they accomplish this, take them out to a kids' media and arcade center.
- Have a spell down. Call out words from the dictionary and take turns trying to spell each one. Winner gets to pick dessert for that evening.
- Read the whole series of Dr. Seuss books in one sitting.
- Locate a baby name book and look up everyone's name and its meaning.
- For one evening, allow your kids to stay up as late as they want.

Fun Together Outside

- Have a bubble blowing contest. Pass out pieces of bubble gum (same number to each person). Practice blowing for a few minutes. Start a timer and see who can blow the biggest bubble in one minute.
- Play flashlight tag on a summer night.
- After a summer rain, go outside to collect earthworms for your favorite fisherman.
- Make jumbo ice cream cones and take them with you on a walk around the neighborhood.

- Roll small balls of chunky peanut butter into birdseed. Place the balls on tree limbs for small animals and birds.
- Wash the car together getting as soapy and wet as possible in the process.
- Set up a lemonade stand.
- Take a walk in the rain (umbrellas optional).
- Sit under a sprinkler on a hot day. See who can stay there the longest.
- Take a midnight walk armed with flashlights and mosquito repellent.
- Plant a tree. Enlist the entire family's help in selecting the type of tree and the site. Take a picture of your family standing around the tree on the same date each year as a reminder of God's faithful provision and promised growth.
- Fill a tub with water balloons. Take it outside and prepare to get wet.
- Climb a tree with your kids. Play "I spy" from the heights.
- Use a telescope to search the skies for familiar constellations. Imagine the stars as works of art and try to form pictures from their positions.
- Weed the yard or garden. Take turns hosing each other off.
- Fill a baby pool with water and dish soap. Use bent hangers to create huge bubbles. Run through the yard to create elongated bubble tunnels.
- Use jumbo sidewalk chalk to create sidewalk gardens, zoos, and murals of your family.
- Have a family fitness night. Do push-ups, pull-ups, jumping jacks, sit-ups, and run around the block.
- Pick out special kites at the store, then fly them as a family.
- Teach your children the games you played as a child. For example: hopscotch, string games, sidewalk tic-tac-toe.
- Bundle up and play flashlight tag on a winter night.
- Lay a blanket outside on the grass. Have everyone lay down and take turns telling stories about the clouds.
- Purchase day-old pies at a discount bread store and have a pie fight.

- Bring out the croquet game and challenge your children to a contest.
- Teach your children how to build a campfire. Be sure to teach fire safety. Roast marshmallows or hot dogs over the open fire.
- Design your own miniature golf course in your yard. Lay empty soup cans on the side for holes. Set up wooden skewers at each hole and attach a piece of construction paper shaped like a triangle with the hole number written on it.
- Pick up acorns, walnuts, and other nuts that fall from the trees. Save these until midwinter, then place a big pile outside a window and watch for the squirrels to come and gather them up.
- Pack and play. Pack a bag lunch for your family. Walk to a nearby park, eat, and then play.
- Have a neighborhood garage and bake sale, proceeds going toward a neighborhood carnival.
- After a few hours of yard work, fill a baby pool with dish soap and warm water. Let everyone sit around soaking their tired feet.

Fun with Food

- Open a box of Oreos and instruct your kids in the fine art of twisting the sides off and savoring each one. Chilled milk for dipping is a must.
- Take back returnable bottles and cans to a store. Then peruse the grocery aisles in search of yummy treats to buy using the refund money.
- Use an old family recipe to bake a cake from scratch. Hand out a knife to everyone and frost it together.
- Make Easter candy suckers by melting candy chips (found in cake decorating departments) and pouring into molds.
- Pick apples at a fruit farm. Come home and teach your kids how to make a homemade apple pie.

- Bring in serving size bowls of clean snow. Pour maple syrup over top. Enjoy homemade snow cones.
- Have a backyard hobo dinner. Dress up like hobos complete with carrying stick and a bandanna filled with eating utensils.
- Bake a batch of potatoes. Invite friends over for a baked potato pot luck. Each family brings a topping for the potatoes.
- Pour M & Ms or Skittles into a large serving bowl. Tell everyone to grab a handful. For every piece of candy taken, each person must provide a compliment about others before eating.
- Make chocolate chip pancakes for dinner. Top with vanilla ice cream and a cherry.
- Buy a family size box of assorted chocolates. Take turns selecting one piece at a time until the box is gone.
- Bring out the fine china. Serve an elegant tea party for your children and their friends.
- Make mud pies. Then clean up and have real chocolate pie for dessert.
- Make grab bags filled with assorted candies and small toys. Keep them tucked away for times when you have to say no to more costly activities.
- Decorate miniature pumpkins with permanent, black markers. Create a whole village of pumpkin people to set out on a front porch or to use as a table display.
- Bob for apples. Wash the apples and push a wooden sucker stick into one end. Dip them in melted caramel.
- Play dinner switch. Kids cook. Mom cleans up.
- Make pizza dough. Shape it into hearts. Let the kids put sauce, toppings, and cheese on their own heart-shaped pizza for Valentine's Day.
- After a hot weather cleanup, cool down with root beer floats.
- Make a Fourth of July cake and decorate it with lighted sparklers.
- Use toothpicks and miniature marshmallows to create a farm house, barn, and fences. Place animal crackers inside fences and barns.

- Create a pudding casserole by layering various flavors of pudding in a large serving bowl. Allow each layer to set before pouring another flavor on top. Hand out large spoons and dig in together.
- Make Popsicles. Freeze grape juice in ice cube trays. Place a Popsicle stick into each space.
- Make rainbow chocolate chip cookies. Separate batter into four bowls. Add different colors of food coloring. Bake as usual.
- Play dress-up with food. Hand out strings of red licorice and assorted circular cereal and candies. String these edible decorations on the licorice strands. Make bracelets, necklaces, or rings. Eat as a snack later on.
- Buy several cans of whipping cream. Take turns making mustaches, beards, eyebrows, and exaggerated lips. Kids can lick off the cream before it droops off.
- Make potato head people. Use toothpicks, olives, raisins, lettuce, and marshmallows to create eyes, mouth, nose, and ears.
- Have a chocolate lunch or dinner. Collect many different chocolate foods to serve for one meal. Include: brownies, cookies, cake, ice cream, pudding, and candy. Don't forget the chocolate milk.
- Save up samples of new food products you receive by mail or purchase single serving sizes at a grocery store. Have a "taste testing" meal. Vote on the best tasting foods.
- Make a batch of bread dough. Twist, braid, and mold the dough into fancy shaped rolls. Sprinkle with poppy seeds, fresh parmesan cheese, or drizzle melted butter over top. Bake and enjoy.
- During a family home movie night, pass out ice cream sundae dishes filled with favorite candies. Serve with a spoon and a smile.
- Make popcorn. Pour it into serving bowls and top with grated parmesan cheese, salted butter, cayenne pepper, or hot caramel sauce.
- Use fun shaped cookie cutters to transform plain lunch meat slices into a fancy feast.
- After you decorate a pumpkin, save the seeds. Rinse them thoroughly, them lay them flat overnight to dry. Place them on a baking sheet,

salt them, and bake on a low setting in an oven for several hours. When they're done, take them out and try them while they're still warm.

- Eat a meal of beans and rice for an entire day. Explain that this type of food is the main diet for many Third World countries.
- Before everyone awakens, get up early and prepare a big breakfast. Set the food on the table, complete with fine china tableware. Let them awaken to the smell of delicious food.

Fun Away from Home

- Call for schedules and costs, then take a bus to another part of town.
- Get a roll of pennies from the bank. Take turns tossing them into a water fountain at a nearby park.
- Go to an indoor ice skating rink on a hot summer day.
- Have a "no-occasion" tailgate party at a local park.
- Get your picture taken at photo booths inside shopping malls. Display the photo strips on your refrigerator. Or, laminate them and use as bookmarks.
- Visit an art museum. Take sketch pads and pencils to try your hand at drawing some of the displays.
- Visit a bakery and sample their wares.
- Tour the astronomy lab at a university.
- Stop by a working fire station. Get a list of fire safety rules for the home, and then draw up a fire escape plan.
- Go to a drive-in movie. Bring your own snacks from home.
- Save all pocket change for one month. Count the money at the month's end and select a place to go as a family.
- Plan a family fun outing costing $10.00 or less.
- Go bird watching at a park. Take along binoculars.
- Hand out $2.00 to each person, and go to garage sales. Each person should find a gift for every family member. Exchange the gifts at home, explaining why the gifts were selected.

- To encourage a young reader, pay your child five cents every time he reads a new word while riding in the car.
- Get out your telephone directory and look for historical sites to visit in your area.
- Go to a local park and rent tandem bikes.
- Visit a working farm and help with the chores.
- In rotation, map out and visit every park and library in your area.
- Take a walk in the woods. Try to identify as many kinds of trees as you can. Take one leaf from each tree home and look in an encyclopedia to identify them.
- Visit your neighborhood park or play area. Bring a box of ice cream cones, a container of ice cream, a scoop, and napkins. Hand out cones to all the children there.
- Get a library card for everyone in your family. Spend one hour a day reading as a family.

Fun Learning Activities

- Create an indoor garden using an old fish bowl or large pickle jar. Fill the jar with potting soil, assorted small plants, and plastic toy figures for display.
- Take a CPR class as a family.
- Get a foreign language book for tourists. Set this book out and only allow communication spoken in the foreign language. Everyone must look up their words before they can speak.
- Layer colored sand in small glass jars. Plant a tiny cactus inside.
- Learn sign language. Demonstrate this new skill for friends and family at a "no-talking" sign language snack party.
- Go fishing. Learn to fillet your catch and cook for dinner.
- Purchase small wooden birdhouses. Paint them and then cover them with outdoor sealant. Hang on tree limbs and watch for birds.
- Learn to make paper airplanes. Have a paper airplane war.

- Begin a stamp collection. Visit the post office for a starter collection.
- String popcorn and cranberries. Hang them outside for a winter treat for birds.
- Learn to fold dinner napkins in fancy ways.
- Create ice candles using small cardboard milk cartons, melted wax, wick, and chipped ice. Place some wicking in the carton (tie the end to a pencil and set horizontally over milk carton top), fill the carton with ice, then pour melted wax over the ice. Hint: melt crayons with wax to create color.
- Go outside with a glass jar and lid. Use tweezers to gently pick up unusual bugs, then look up information on the insects.
- Make thumbprint animal pictures. Use stamp pads and thumbs.
- Train a guide dog for the blind.
- Pick wildflowers. Hang flowers upside down in a dark closet until completely dry. Spray with acrylic clear coating. Arrange in a basket or hang from a peg.
- Gather seashells and sand into a bucket. Make a fist-sized indentation, place a wick into the hole (tie one end of the wick to a pencil and lay the pencil horizontally across the top), and fill with melted wax—instant sand candles, complete with decorative shells.
- Create a family tree on poster board. Place a photo of each person above their name on the chart.
- Learn to change both a tire and the oil in the car. Do it as a family.
- Ask for old flowers from a florist. Dry the petals on a flat surface. Add a few drops of fragrant oil, and mix. Cut six-inch squares of mesh material. Fill the mesh with dried flowers. Secure with a ribbon. Give them away as drawer sachets.
- Have an empathy day. Pretend each family member is disabled, use an eye patch, tie an arm down to the side, put cotton in ears, use crutches to walk, etc. Children will better understand those with real disabilities once they've spent an entire day with their own pretend disability.
- Make up a first-aid kit for your home and each car.

- Teach basic mending skills. Sew on missing buttons and hem up loose edges on pants, skirts, or dresses.
- Select books at the library for family members to read to each other.
- Borrow a hair cutting instruction video. Be brave and cut your children's hair.
- Collect in a mesh fruit bag colorful ribbon, thread, yarn, and strips of cloth. Hang the mesh bag outside for the birds to use for their nests. Watch colorful bird nests appear!
- Purchase a flower pot and some grout. Spread the grout evenly over the flower pot, and press in various trinkets or memorabilia like marbles, sea shells, or coins. Let dry. Try making a bird bath using the same method.
- Play dictionary stump. Each person finds a difficult word. Others must try and guess its meaning. These words can be acted out in charade-like fashion.
- Practice first-aid skills such as treating burns, cuts, and broken bones.
- Get out a road map. Teach your kids how to read it and estimate arrival time.
- Teach your children how to iron a shirt.
- Purchase wooden yo-yos at a craft supply store. Decorate them with paints. Once they're dry, practice tricks using these "old-fashioned" yo-yos.
- Plan a fix-it day. Bring all broken toys to the kitchen. Get out basic tools like hammers, nails, screws, electrical tape, etc. Try to repair each one.
- Demonstrate the proper way to introduce new acquaintances and how to respond to these introductions.
- Use the Internet to "travel" by looking up far away places and learn more about foreign lands and people.
- Borrow a line-dancing instructional video and practice together.
- Though they may never use it, show your son how to bow, your daughter how to curtsy.

- Teach your children the principle of tithing using ten dimes. Mark paper cups with the words: tithe, save, and spend. Allow your children to practice by dropping the coins into each cup.
- Take a ceramics class before Christmas. Make and decorate new Christmas ornaments for display and to give as gifts.
- Get a video on self-defense and practice the skills as a family.
- Help your children develop entrepreneurial skills by encouraging them to create a home business or service for friends and neighbors.
- Combine learning with fun—rent or borrow biographical movies for a rainy day.

Fun Serving Others

- Raid your kitchen cupboards for non-favorites. Take these foodstuffs to the nearest food shelter or contribute to your church's food pantry.
- Rake leaves for a neighbor. Don't forget to stop and have a leaf fight every five minutes.
- Clean out storage areas. Bundle up unwanted items for local thrift shops and deliver them.
- Surprise the neighbors and build a snowman in their yard.
- Set out the hot cocoa, enjoy a cup and then bundle up and go rake leaves or shovel snow for an elderly neighbor.
- Send "we appreciate you" cards to your family's doctors, dentists, teachers, pastors, and youth workers.
- Trade household chores for the day. Mom does the kids' chores and vice versa.
- Bake Valentine's Day cookies for nursing home residents.
- Design Christmas cards and send them to the veterans at a VA hospital. Include a family photo in the envelope for nurses to pass around to patients so they can put faces to the names on the cards your family created.
- Send out "thank you for being you" cards to faithful friends.

- Adopt your neighborhood. Wear gloves and bring large garbage bags to pick up roadside garbage.
- Write a family letter, each person contributing a paragraph, to distant relatives. Address envelopes, make copies of the letter, and send.
- Write down scripture promises on pieces of paper. Insert one promise into a balloon. Blow up the balloons and let them go outdoors. Send up a prayer or promise that will bring encouragement to the person who finds the balloon.
- Purchase plastic Easter eggs. Fill them with candy and a resurrection scripture verse. Hand out the eggs to neighborhood children.
- Create a circulating home video. Tape a video of your family. Send it to out of town family members with a list of other extended family and their addresses.
- Groom a cat or dog. Ask a neighbor with an animal to let you assist him or her if you don't own a pet.
- Offer to do some spring cleaning for an elderly neighbor. Bring a midday snack to share with your host.
- Take a day to fast and pray for someone in need. Explain to your children the biblical principle of combining fasting and prayer.
- Put everyone's name in a hat. Pass the hat around and have each person takes a name. For the entire weekend, play secret slave to the person whose name you've drawn. Do as many chores and nice things as you can during those two days.
- Bring a friend home for lunch. Ask each child to invite a friend over for a simple lunch and to play for the afternoon.
- Pick and pray. Have each child pick out one person from church to pray for during the upcoming week. Each night before bed, every one should spend five minutes praying for that person.
- As your children get older, offer to baby-sit for an infant. Teach your children how to care for the special needs of a baby. Practice holding properly, diapering, and feeding the baby.

- Allow your children to teach neighborhood kids simple crafts at an afternoon craft class in your home.
- Allow your children to plan and host a tea party along with their friends for their moms.